INCREDIBLE
EDIBLES

INCREDIBLE
EDIBLES

MATTHEW BIGGS

Contents

Introduction

In our increasingly connected world we are regularly introduced to exciting new cuisines and unfamiliar foodstuffs from across the globe. We are eager to recreate that dish we enjoyed at the restaurant last night, taste again those amazing fruits we discovered on holiday, or try out that new superfood we read about online.

At the same time, more and more of us are breaking free from supermarket conformity and the limited choices offered by industrial-scale food production. We are discovering once again the joys of diversity in fruit and veg, and unearthing forgotten crops from closer to home.

Our eyes have been opened to a new world of previously unknown food crops with exciting flavours and often supercharged health benefits. Yet it can be a struggle to find the right ingredients and where they are available they can often be prohibitively expensive.

So what to do? There's nothing else for it but to grow your own! And thankfully another benefit of our globalised world is that so many exotic and obscure crops are now widely available to buy as seeds, tubers, and container-raised plants.

By growing your own incredible edibles, not only will you reap the mental and physical benefits of gardening – fresh air, relaxation, and gentle exercise – but the crops you harvest will be at their peak of quality, full of flavour and packed with nutrients. And you can grow them in the quantities you desire, turning a superfood treat into an everyday delight.

The opportunity to grow crops is open to everyone, no matter what little space you have. Whether in pots on a windowsill, in containers on a balcony, in a courtyard allotment, or in a tiny strip of a garden, from inner city to suburb there is always room to grow your own.

And don't be discouraged if you've never gardened before. With a little attention, most of the crops in this book are easy to grow and all come with detailed step-by-step instructions and advice. For the absolute beginners among you I've provided a crash course in cultivating plants in the pages *Tips and techniques for growing*.

Whatever your level of experience, I believe everyone should try to grow one or two new crops a year. One of the joys of being alive is finding something new to get excited about. With 58 remarkable crops to discover in the pages of this book, don't just grow and eat the same-old – make it incredible!

Matthew Biggs

Tips and techniques for growing

Take time to understand your growing space and the conditions needed by each crop, so you can select what will flourish and prepare the ground. Then it's a matter of sowing or planting, tending to the needs of the crops as you watch them grow, and reaping the delicious rewards.

Deciding what to grow

Faced with so many fascinating options, you probably want to try growing them all, but it's worth pausing to consider the following questions. Be practical in assessing what you can manage, and then browse through the crop choosers on pp.14–19, to help you decide.

The lavender flowers of society garlic are both beautiful to look at and powerfully flavoured.

What would I like to grow?

Crops for the table It sounds obvious, but grow crops that you are keen to eat. Use the Cook's tips panels to match crops to your tastes. Those that are unavailable or expensive in shops, or that simply taste better freshly picked, are especially worth growing.

Crops for the eye Every edible plant has aesthetic appeal too. Plan to create displays of contrasting leaf colour and texture, bold flowers, shapely fruits, and architectural form.

Do I have enough space?

Grow in pots Limited space? No soil? Containers are the answer. Given drainage holes and space for roots, anything can be grown in pots. Square containers make efficient use of space and those with handles or wheels can be moved from sun to shade.

Grow up Use vertical space by training climbing plants up walls, fences, and other supports.

Grow indoors Use a windowsill to raise seedlings. Given sunlight and large pots, many of the tender crops in this book will happily grow indoors.

Catch-crop Sow fast-growing crops between those that germinate slowly, or hardier crops while waiting to plant out tender crops.

Work in edibles Find space in existing ornamental borders to grow edibles. Perennial crops and shrubs can make attractive permanent features.

If you don't have a pond grow water-loving crops such as water celery in a metal container.

Do I have the time and inclination?

Start small There's no need to aim for perfection or self-sufficiency. It's better to enjoy growing a few crops well than have the burden of maintaining too many. Grow more as you gain experience.

Little-and-often Even the busiest people can find time to grow edibles. The key to keeping on top of things is to check plants and carry out jobs as frequently as you can. And there are numerous time-saving techniques (see *Reduce the workload*, opposite).

Horticultural fleece protects plants from frost as well as pests such as caterpillars.

Consider growing in raised beds if drainage or soil quality is poor.

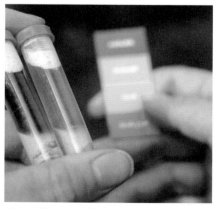

Check if your soil is acid or alkaline and tailor your planting accordingly.

Do I have the right growing conditions?

General climate Plants that hail from a climate similar to your own are more likely to thrive with minimal input. Cooler areas have a shorter frost-free growing season, so outdoor sowing is done later and tender crops may need protection to reach maturity. Latitude also affects day length, which influences when some crops will be ready to harvest.

Sun and shade Edible crops generally prefer full sun, so note how much sun your garden gets during the day and at different times of year, and choose the sunniest spot for them. Make use of heat radiating from sunny walls.

Wind and frost Both make growing difficult and should be avoided as much as possible. Wind damages plants and chills the ground, while frost lingers in shady corners and at the bottom of slopes, and can kill off seedlings and tender plants. Use shelter from existing walls or trees, and add a permeable barrier, like a hedge, to allow cold air to drain through.

Rainfall In regions with low rainfall, and where soil is dry at the base of walls and fences, installing drip irrigation provides a consistent supply of moisture. Digging in organic matter, such as garden compost, will improve the moisture-holding capacity of soil. Where rainfall is high, raised beds improve drainage.

Soil type Soil composition influences how it drains and holds nutrients. All soils benefit from the addition of organic matter, and you can improve the drainage of clay soil by digging in horticultural sand or grit. Check whether your soil is acid, alkaline, or neutral with a simple pH test kit. If it is highly acidic, add lime to increase the pH and grow acid-loving plants like the tea shrub. Where soil is poor or full of rubble, the easiest solution is to create raised beds or grow in containers.

Reduce the workload

Don't waste time in the garden with unnecessary work. Try these top labour-saving tips:

■ Plant through a plastic mulch or apply a thick organic mulch around plants (above) to reduce the need for weeding and watering.

■ Plant densely to crowd out weeds.

■ Buy annuals as young plants if you've no time to raise from seed.

■ Grow perennial crops, such as skirret and Chilean guava, which are usually less work than annuals.

■ Install an automatic drip irrigation system (below) to save watering; especially useful for containers.

continued »

Growing from seed

Growing your own plants from seed is satisfying and fun: you will never lose the childlike pleasure of seeing the first green shoots peeping through the soil. It is also easy to do if you follow the step-by-step guides so that each crop is given the conditions it needs to get off to the best start. Investing in specialist equipment, such as a heated propagator and soil thermometer, is worthwhile and improves the chance of success.

Smaller seeds can be sown thickly in shallow trays, but must be potted on individually as soon as they can be handled.

Sow large seeds in individual pots filled with compost, inserting one seed per pot and covering it over.

Sowing indoors

Indoor sowing can be done anywhere light and warm, such as a greenhouse, conservatory, or on a windowsill. It's a great way to give hardy crops a head start and extend the growing season for tender crops in colder climates. Sow into clean containers filled with good quality soil-based or organic seed compost. Water with tepid tap water and keep in a lidded propagator (ideally heated) at 18–20°C (64–68°F), unless instructions state otherwise.

Sowing small seeds Fill a shallow seed tray with compost. Mix the seeds with fine dry sand and sow thinly over the surface. Sieve a thin layer of compost or vermiculite over the seeds and water using a watering can with a fine rose. Once large enough to handle, transplant the seedlings into larger pots or cellular trays by easing the roots out with a dibber and holding the seed leaves.

Sowing larger seeds For medium-sized seeds, sow 2 seeds per module of a cellular tray or root-trainer, cover lightly with compost, and water. Once germinated, remove the weakest seedling, then transplant when the first roots are visible through drainage holes in the base. Sow and transplant large seeds in the same way, but sow individually into 9cm (3½in) pots by pressing them down into the compost.

Heated propagators

Constant heat produces the quickest, most reliable germination and it is worth investing in a heated propagator for early sowing, as temperatures in unheated propagators and airing cupboards fluctuate. Buy one large enough to suit your needs, ideally with a digital thermostat for accurate temperature control and even germination; the cost will be repaid through less wasted seed and at harvest time.

Acclimatizing plants

If you have ever jumped into a cold bath then you'll know what it's like for a young plant taken straight from a greenhouse to S a cold, breezy veg plot: the shock is enough to check growth or even kill it. Plants raised under cover must be acclimatized gradually in a process called "hardening off".

How to harden off

Week 1 - Leave seedlings outside during the day covered with 2 layers of fleece. Bring in at night.

Week 2 - Reduce to 1 layer of fleece. Near the end of the week, remove fleece during the day and, if it's not too cold, leave plants out at night but covered.

Week 3 - Towards the end of the week, leave uncovered day and night before planting out. Be ready with fleece if frost is forecast.

Alternatively, place plants in a cold frame – a wooden box with a hinged glass lid – and prop the lid open during the day, progressively wider, shutting it again at night, until the lid is left fully open day and night in week 3.

A cold frame is a useful structure for hardening off young plants.

Sourcing seeds

All the unusual crops in this book are available from seed merchants and specialist suppliers on the internet, but explore other sources too. Chickpeas, fenugreek, taro, amaranth, and turmeric can be found in Asian grocers, while society garlic and hostas are grown by specialist nurseries. Save seed from your own crops by allowing them to flower and shaking the dry pods or seedheads into a paper bag or envelope in summer. Then take part in "seed swaps", which are a great chance to meet and chat with enthusiastic growers and discover something new. I first discovered achocha and an amaranthus simply labelled 'Tower Hamlets' (a borough of London) at a seed swap.

Sowing outdoors

Seed can also be sown directly outdoors into a prepared seedbed. React to the weather each season rather than relying on seed packet instructions for when to sow. Seeds will not germinate in cold, wet weather. Wait until the soil is warm and moist - invest in a soil thermometer to check - and germination will be quicker and more consistent.

Prepare the seedbed Improve the soil as described overleaf, then level it by raking in two directions at 90 degrees. Cover with polythene to warm and hoe off any weed seedlings.

Sow in drills Rake again before sowing. Make a drill by pushing a length of bamboo cane on to the surface of the soil, or drawing along the corner of a rake. Water the drill before sowing and sprinkle seed thinly into the bottom. Lightly cover with soil and label with plant name and date.

As you rake, remove debris such as large and medium stones.

continued »

Planting and general care

Moving new plants to their final positions is a satisfying moment. To help them establish quickly, it's important to prepare the growing site properly and plant out new arrivals with care. Plants grown in open soil are often good at looking after themselves, but a little regular watering, feeding, and weeding will spur them on. Don't forget that crops in pots and under cover are totally reliant on you for water and nutrients.

Preparing the site

Make life easy for yourself by providing crops with their preferred soil conditions. Most crops love a moisture-retentive, free-draining soil with an open structure full of air spaces, a bit like a bath sponge.

Improving the soil Clear the site of weeds and remove any larger stones and other debris, before digging in plenty of well-rotted organic matter, such as manure, compost, or leaf mould. Spread it thickly over the planting site and then thoroughly mix into the soil using a garden fork. Heavy clay will also benefit from the addition of sharp sand or horticultural grit and gypsum to improve drainage. Give the soil a few days to settle before planting.

Using raised beds Easy to maintain and a great way to bring in good soil where yours is poor, raised beds can be built very simply using recycled scaffolding boards or similar planks, fixed in place with stakes.

■ Leave access paths between beds.
■ Orientate east-west (or the reverse in the southern hemisphere) for optimum sunlight.
■ Raise to a height that suits you and your crops.
■ Make them a maximum of 3m (10ft) long and a width that's a comfortable reach, to avoid standing on soil.

As well as being dug into the soil, a thick layer of well-rotted organic matter can be spread over the surface to act as a mulch.

A typical raised bed is 15cm (6in) deep. If your crops need netting, leave long corner stakes as a ready-made frame.

Growing under cover

In cooler climates, glasshouses extend the growing season in spring and autumn, and raise temperatures in summer, making it possible to obtain harvests from more tender crops.

Site glasshouses to receive light throughout the day and make sure the roof vents are equivalent to 15–20 per cent of floor area to moderate summer temperatures. Opening vents allows insect pollinators access to flowering plants, but hand pollination may still be necessary. Cold frames, mini greenhouses, and cloches (below) are also handy for raising seedlings, hardening off young plants, and protecting new transplants.

Planting out

Transferring plants to their final growing position is a critical time. Harden them off if raised under cover (see p.11) and treat gently to prevent damage. Always water plants in pots before transplanting; adding liquid seaweed helps to reduce shock.

How to plant Dig a hole slightly larger than the rootball. Water the base of the hole if dry and sprinkle in mycorrhizal fungi to help increase the absorptive area of the plant's roots. Ease the rootball from the pot, place in the hole at a depth so that the soil surface matches the level of the compost, then gently firm the soil around it. Water in well, add any supports required, and shelter with fleece until established.

Before planting, gently tease out the roots to help the plant establish.

Aftercare

Ensuring that your crops are kept clean, warm, well fed, and watered can mean the difference between success and failure.

Watering Thoroughly soak soil around the base of plants (not the leaves) to encourage roots to grow down into the soil in search of moisture. If given a trickle, roots will stay near the surface and dessicate quickly. Watering during the evening in summer reduces evaporation.

Feeding Don't encourage soft growth with high-nitrogen feeds; use a balanced general fertilizer, seaweed tonic, or high-potash tomato feed to encourage flowering and fruiting. Acid-loving plants like tea need a specialist feed.

Weeding Weeds compete for moisture, nutrients, and light, so keep crops weed-free. A thick mulch of 5–7.5cm (2–3in) of well-rotted organic matter or composted bark, spread over moist, weed-free soil effectively suppresses them. Always remove weeds before they flower and set seed.

Protection Cold winds, frost, and scorching sunlight can all damage plants. Use horticultural fleece to cover and protect crops from frost. Thick mulches and cloches also provide frost protection, while high temperatures can be mitigated using shade from netting.

Water generously near the base of the stem to encourage root growth.

Use a hoe to remove weeds between plants, or a hand fork around stems.

Growing in pots

Choose the largest pots possible and ensure root crops have enough depth to grow well. Plastic pots hold moisture better and can be dropped inside terracotta pots to improve their appearance. Always make sure there is a drainage hole at the base, and cover the hole with pieces of broken pots or large stones to stop the hole getting clogged with soil.

Use a compost mix of 80 per cent loam-based to 20 per cent multi-purpose, which is easier to rewet if it dries out. Keep plants well watered when in growth, and consider using an automatic irrigation system if you're busy or often away. Feed plants regularly and repot perennials or replace the top layer of compost in their pot annually to keep them growing strongly.

Choose your crops

Wonderful as it would be to grow all these amazing crops in one go, it is more practical to start with a few. These pages pick out plants suited to particular growing conditions or ambitions, so you can make the perfect match.

CROPS FOR POTS

If you have limited space, these plants will work particularly well in containers. Many edibles thrive in pots, given the proper care. Containers are a great way to keep tender crops portable, too, if they need to be brought under cover in cold weather.

Sweetleaf The leaves of this tender perennial are the source of the sugar substitute Stevia – *see p.180*.

Turkish orange aubergine A compact crop that makes a decorative pot plant with its glorious orange fruits – *see p.26*.

Shiso Attractive, cinnamon-scented Japanese herb with wrinkled burgundy or bright green foliage – *see p.54*.

Tea An evergreen, acid-loving shrub, tea plants are best grown in pots if your soil is alkaline – *see p.178*.

Hyacinth beans Where summers are cool, grow this purple-podded legume in large pots under cover – *see p.30*.

Cape gooseberry Heart-shaped leaves and fruit enclosed in papery lanterns make for an attractive pot specimen – *see p.198*.

Also try

■ **Yam bean** Large pots suit this vigorous Mexican vine, grown for its white-fleshed tubers – *see p.116*.

■ **Turmeric** A heat-loving Asian spice, grown for its boldly flavoured and coloured rhizomes and large, attractive, edible leaves – *see p.166*.

■ **Finger lime** A citrus shrub native to Australia and best grown in containers to move outdoors in summer and back indoors in autumn – *see p.188*.

FAST-GROWING CROPS

Edibles that race from germination to harvest in just a few weeks are ideal if you can't wait to try your new crops. Choose from this selection for maximum productivity or where space is at a premium, or if you need vigorous climbers to rapidly clothe walls or fences.

Chrysanthemum greens The feather-like leaves of this easy-to-grow green have a strongly herbal taste – *see p.76*.

Red orach Sow every few weeks as a cut-and-come-again salad crop or let it grow tall for mature leaves – *see p.60*.

Fenugreek The aromatic leaves of this annual plant are quick to crop, and seeds can be harvested later – *see p.154*.

Rat-tail radishes Grown for their spicy, pointed pods, these radishes quickly grow over 1m (3ft) tall – *see p.56*.

Achocha Vigorous vine producing prolific crops of pods with a taste of cucumber and sweet pepper – *see p.48*.

Callaloo Grown as a cut-and-come-again crop, baby leaves of callaloo can be ready to pick 3–4 weeks after sowing – *see p.80*.

Hardy passion fruit A tough, rampant climber that drips with heavy crops of summer fruits – *see p.206*.

Also try
■ **Snake gourd** The cylindrical fruits of this squash are eaten like courgettes when young or can be allowed to reach great lengths – *see p.22*.

■ **Hyacinth beans** A vigorous climbing bean with pretty flowers and delicious purple pods – *see p.30*.

■ **Salsola** Also know as "saltwort", the slender, succulent leaves of this saltmarsh plant are a sought-after delicacy in Italy and Japan, and grow well in alkaline soil – *see p.88*.

SHADE-LOVING CROPS

Every garden has a shady corner, but there is no need to struggle to fill it. Plenty of the crops in this book are woodlanders in the wild, which thrive given shelter from the heat of the sun.

Wood sorrel Dainty and elegant ground cover; the trefoil leaves of this spreading plant taste of sharp apples – *see p.158*.

White alpine strawberry For evergreen ground cover and a steady supply of tiny, sweet, white berries – *see p.212*.

Sushi hosta Shoots, leaves, and stems of hostas are all edible and are a favourite vegetable in Japan – *see p.70*.

Oregon grape The blue berries borne in late summer by these evergreen shrubs make lovely preserves – *see p.210*.

Chokeberry Attractive shrubs bearing white flowers, deep purple berries, and rich autumn colour – *see p.204*.

Japanese hardy ginger Cold-tolerant species of ginger grown for its tender stems and flower buds – *see p.174*.

Fish mint The heart-shaped leaves of this perennial have a unique, slightly fishy, orange-coriander flavour – *see p.162*.

Also try

■ **Ostrich ferns** Shade-lovers, these statuesque ferns produce fronds up to 1m (3ft) tall. As the fronds unfurl in spring, their coiled ends can be picked and eaten – *see p.68*.

■ **Fuchsia berry** Following their showy, ballerina flowers, all fuchsias bear plentiful, sweet-tasting berries, but make sure you choose a cultivar known for its fruits – *see p.196*.

CROPS FOR BOGGY GROUND

Wet soil is not traditionally used in gardens to cultivate edible plants, but with this selection of crops there is no reason why a pond margin or bog garden can't be productive as well as beautiful.

Skirret This ancient root vegetable has a taste reminiscent of parsnip and carrot with a hint of pepper – *see p.122*.

Ostrich ferns Happiest planted in shade by a pond, the tips of their unfurling fronds are a spring delicacy – *p.68*.

Meadowsweet This moisture-loving plant produces a foam of edible flowers with the flavour of almonds – *see p.182*.

Camas Long, slow cooking turns the bulbs of these blue-flowered perennials into an edible delicacy – *see p.96*.

Chinese artichoke Grown for its knobbly tubers, this perennial also has attractive mint-like foliage – *see p.106*.

Wasabi The roots of this slow-growing perennial are the source of the potent green paste served with sushi – *see p.170*.

Water celery True to its name, this ground cover perennial with celery-flavoured leaves thrives in wet soil – *see p.164*.

Also try

■ **Fish mint** A popular ornamental that flourishes in wet soils, few growers realise its leaves can be used as a herb in Asian cooking – *see p.162*.

■ **Taro** This tropical crop is grown for its sweet-potato-like corms and large, edible leaves, and loves to be kept wet at the roots – *see p.112*.

■ **Mashua** The spicy tubers of this South American crop need constant moisture to plump up – *see p.102*.

CROPS FOR SMALL GARDENS

Compact growth can be helpful when space is limited, but tall and climbing plants also take up little soil space and add interesting vertical elements to a display.

Honeyberry The dusty-blue berries of this compact shrub are packed with vitamin C and antioxidants – *see p.194*.

Dahlia yam Yes, you read it right: the tubers of many dahlias have a deliciously nutty flavour – *see p.98*.

Chilean guava With fruits like strawberry and bubblegum, this petite, unfussy shrub deserves a spot in any garden – *see p.190*.

Strawberry popcorn A miniature maize variety that produces small cobs of red kernels for popping – *see p.148*.

Electric daisies The edible flowers of these bushy plants produce a pleasantly tingling sensation – *see p.50*.

Daylilies The buds, trumpet-like flowers, stems, shoots, and roots of this ornamental perennial are all edible – *see p.130*.

Asparagus peas Given support, this spreading plant takes up little space and bears tasty, winged pods – *see p.38*.

Also try

■ **Chia** Upright, but not spreading, the tall blue flowers spikes of chia will add height to a small garden, and are followed by a crop of superfood seeds – *see p.142*.

■ **Mashua** A real multi-purpose plant, mashua is a bushy climber with pretty, grey-green leaves and bright flowers, all of which are edible, along with the crisp and spicy tubers – *see p.102*.

DROUGHT-TOLERANT CROPS

Plants that can withstand dry periods and still produce a harvest are unusual, but some of these tough crops can do just that. This makes them ideal for gardens in dry climates or on lighter, free-draining soils.

Goji berry These hardy shrubs withstand wind, drought, and salt-laden air to produce prolific crops of berries - *see p.202*.

Huauzontle Once established, huauzontle tolerates heat and drought to produce tender, broccoli-like flower heads - *see p.86*.

Yacón This towering plant, with crisp, pear-flavoured tubers, survives drought better than most root crops - *see p.92*.

Chickpeas The roots of this legume probe deep into the soil in search of water, making it a less thirsty crop - *see p.34*.

Strawberry spinach A long taproot ensures good drought resistance and great yields of leaves and fruits - *see p.72*.

Amaranth Varieties of amaranth grown mainly for their seeds crop better when watered sparingly - *see p.136*.

Quinoa This easy-care annual, grown for its protein-rich seeds, requires watering only in severe drought - *see p.140*.

Also try
■ **Earth chestnut** This pretty, white-flowered perennial needs almost no watering once established, and produces tubers with a taste like chestnuts when cooked, leaves similar to parsley, and seeds like smoky cumin - *see p.118*.

■ **Sesame** The familiar burger-bun seeds come from a glorious flowering plant, similar to a foxglove, which needs high temperatures to thrive - *see p.146*.

FRUITING VEGETABLES

Level 2
moderate

Snake gourd

Trichosanthes cucumerina var. anguina

Squashes grow in a diverse range of colours and sizes, and find expression in the fantastic shapes of their fruits. Snake gourds are no exception, producing long, cylindrical fruits, which, left to their own devices, will coil up like a bed spring – or, indeed, like a snake wrapped around a tree branch.

What is it?

Snake gourds are fast-growing climbing vines believed to have originated in tropical Southeast Asia. The white, star-shaped flowers, with long, curly frills to the petal edges and a deliciously sweet fragrance, are rather small and delicate considering the supersized fruit that develop from them. Young fruits can be prepared and eaten in their entirety, like courgettes, while the red pulp of mature fruits makes a good substitute for tomatoes. Young shoots and leaves are also edible and, although all parts of the plant taste bitter when raw, this disappears after cooking. If you've got kids (or even if you haven't) leave a few mature specimens to paint up and turn into colourful vegetable snakes.

To produce the longest, straightest gourds, some growers harness the power of gravity by tying weights to the ends of developing fruits.

Plants bear both male and female flowers, and for fruits to form male pollen must be transferred to female flowers.

How do I grow it?

Given their tropical heritage, in cooler climates it pays to start plants off early under cover and plant them out in a warm, sunny spot in the garden. Snake gourds are vigorous climbers and you will need to provide them with some sort of sturdy climbing frame to scramble over; a pergola is ideal. And, assuming you want to grow a few long, straight, mature specimens, whatever structure you choose should be at least 1.5m (5ft) tall, since the fruits will coil if they touch the ground.

Fruits of the longest varieties can extend up to 1.5m (5ft) but are best eaten when still under 45cm (18in) in length.

Quick guide

In cooler climates sow indoors in spring at 25-30°C (77-86°F)

Some like it hot! Minimum temperature needed for growth is 20°C (68°F)

Grow in a sheltered, sunny site outdoors, in rich, moist, well-drained soil

Keep moist but avoid waterlogging

Vines can spread up to 5m (16ft)

Harvest long varieties at about 45cm (18in); smaller types around 20cm (8in)

Step-by-step growing ≫

Step-by-step growing

To produce a good crop of fruits, snake gourd needs warm conditions in a sheltered site, with free-draining soil, rich in organic matter, and regular watering throughout the growing season.

When to grow and harvest
Start sowing indoors in spring and harvest the fruits when they are still young.

	early winter	late winter	early spring	late spring	early summer	late summer	early autumn	late autumn
sow indoors			●	●				
plant out				●	●			
harvest					●	●	●	

1 Sow indoors

In spring, sow seeds individually into 9.5cm (4in) pots filled with moist, multi-purpose compost. Sow seeds vertically 5mm (¼in) deep. Keep in a propagator heated at 25–30°C (77–86°F) until they germinate, which should be within 2 to 3 weeks. When the first couple of leaves have appeared, transplant the seedlings into individual pots one size larger and grow on. Harden off the young plants once all danger of frost has passed (see p.62).

Grow on seedlings in fresh compost and place in a bright position.

2 Plant out

Plant the young snake gourds at the same level as they were in their pots, and about 60 cm (2ft) apart. Then form a raised circular ridge of soil about 7.5cm (3in) high, encircling the base of each plant. Always water within this circular area, so that moisture will soak down to the roots rather than draining away. Protect from early cold snaps with horticultural fleece or cloches, and feed with a general fertilizer until they are growing well.

Snake gourd is a hungry crop and needs a rich soil to thrive.

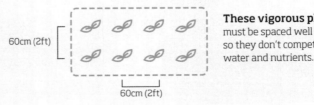

60cm (2ft)

60cm (2ft)

These vigorous plants must be spaced well apart so they don't compete for water and nutrients.

③ Train and prune

Provide a sturdy climbing frame for plants in the form of strong trellis or a pergola, or by building a large frame using stout canes or poles and covering it with netting; the structure should be at least 1.5m (5ft) tall. Train the stems up the vertical supports by tying them in regularly, and allow them to spread over the top.

Prune out the sideshoots of each plant until it has reached the top of the climbing frame; this will help improve yields by directing energy towards fruiting.

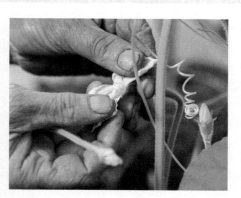

④ Care and harvest

Once plants begin to flower, switch to a high-potash feed. Pollination by insects can be erratic and it may be better to cross-pollinate flowers by hand. Take a male flower and tap pollen from its anthers on to the receptive parts of female flowers, which have small, embryonic fruits at their base. Harvest long varieties once they reach 45cm (18in), smaller types at about 20cm (8in).

Cook's tips

Keep fresh

Keep young snake gourds in the fridge and use within a few days of harvesting. Larger fruits can be stored in a cool, dry place for several months.

How to eat

Young fruits can be steamed or sautéed like courgettes, and substituted for them in recipes. Pick and eat only young fruits as mature gourds develop a bitter taste.

- Slice finely and marinate with salt, sugar, white wine vinegar and dill as a refreshing side.

- Chop and stir-fry with curry leaves and mustard seeds for a simple South Indian-style dish.

- Deep-fry snake gourd dipped in a chickpea flour batter and serve with a fresh coriander or tamarind chutney.

- Chop the snake gourd into 5cm (2in) lengths, scoop out the centre, and stuff with a mince or bean stew before baking.

How to preserve

Combine surplus fruits with runner beans in a chutney, or slice, salt, and cover with sweetened and spiced vinegar to make a pickle.

Level 3
advanced

Turkish orange aubergine

Solanum melongena x S. torvum

A remarkable heirloom variety of aubergine from a country that invented some of the finest aubergine dishes in the world. Perfect for growing in pots, the compact plants produce plentiful crops of sweet, well-flavoured fruits with glossy, orange-and-green striped skins that mature to pure orange and red.

What is it?

Aubergines grow as perennial plants in warm regions, annuals in cooler climes. Some varieties form bushes as tall as 2.5m (8ft); the Turkish orange is a more modest affair, growing to a small but sturdy 60cm (24in). What it lacks in stature, it makes up for in productivity, and bushes often end up heaving with fruits. A relative of tomatoes and peppers, the ancestry of aubergines is somewhat mysterious, but they may have originated in India, where wild forms are found.

Moorish invaders brought the fruit to Spain – "aubergine" is a corruption of the Arabic al-badingan – and the Spanish took them to the New World.

Flowers are "buzz pollinated", waiting for the correct wing frequency of visiting bees before releasing their pollen.

How do I grow it?

Aubergines need a long growing season and prefer continuous warm weather throughout their lives, thriving in tropical and mid-temperate climates. In cooler areas, it is best to start seeds off under cover early in the year, keeping them at a steady temperature of 20–30°C (68–86°F). Then either continue growing plants under cover in medium-sized pots, a border in a greenhouse, or in growing bags, or, where outside temperatures are warm enough, transplant into large pots and grow in a sunny, sheltered site. Pollination can sometimes be haphazard, especially if grown indoors where the bees may not get at the flowers so easily. If this is a problem, you can take on the role of pollinator yourself by gently tapping the flowers or using a fine brush.

The **tomato-like fruits** start off green, before developing orange stripes and turning fully orange when ripe.

Quick guide

Sow under cover from midwinter and move outside after the last frosts

22-30°C (72-86°F) is ideal; growth minimal below 17°C (63°F) and above 35°C (95°F)

Grow in a sheltered, sunny position, in moist, warm, free-draining soil

Keep well watered, using tepid water

Grows up to 60cm (24in) high and 45cm (18in) across

Pick fruits when the skin is glossy; overripe fruit is matt in appearance

Step-by-step growing »

Step-by-step growing

Aubergines need warmth, sunshine, and regular feeding and watering to flourish. Most varieties only thrive outdoors in a hot climate and otherwise need the protection of growing under glass.

When to grow and harvest

Late winter is the perfect time to begin sowing seeds and will give plants the longest possible growing season.

	early winter	late winter	early spring	late spring	early summer	late summer	early autumn	late autumn
sow indoors		•	•					
plant out				•	•			
harvest						•	•	

① Sow indoors

In late winter, around 8 to 10 weeks before the last frosts in your area, sow seeds in pots or modules of moist seed compost in a propagator or airing cupboard at around 18–21°C (64–70°F) and lightly cover. The temperature is important, as the seeds may not germinate if it is too low. Once the seedlings are large enough to handle, transplant them into larger pots, and then again if they start to outgrow those.

Using a dibber to pot on seedlings helps protect the roots from damage.

② Plant on

By late spring or early summer, the aubergine plants should be large enough to transfer to their final growing position. If you live in a warm climate, plant outdoors in a sheltered, sunny spot; otherwise, move them to a greenhouse border. Space plants around 50–60cm (20–24in) apart. If you are growing them in containers, plant them individually in 20–30cm (8–12in) pots of multi-purpose compost.

A warm, sheltered spot is the most important requirement when growing aubergines.

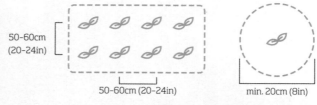

50–60cm (20–24in)

50–60cm (20–24in)

min. 20cm (8in)

Grow in rows 50–60cm (20–24in) apart, or singly in containers or growing bags.

③ Aftercare

Stake and tie in the main stem as it grows. When plants reach around 30cm (12in) in height, pinch out or cut off the growing tip to encourage branching and fruiting. Feed with general fertilizer according to the manufacturer's instructions until established, then switch to tomato fertilizer once the first fruits have formed. Mist the foliage regularly with tepid water to discourage two-spotted mite. Water as soon as the compost surface starts to dry out. Allow access for pollinating insects if growing under cover. You can encourage fruit set by vibrating open flowers with your fingers.

Stake and tie in plants as they grow to keep them well supported.

④ Thin out and harvest

Where you have a cluster of four or more fruits, it's worth removing one or two of the smaller fruits to help the others ripen and achieve a good size. Harvest fruits once they have turned a glossy red colour. Compost plants at the end of the growing season.

Hyacinth beans

Level 2 *moderate*

Lablab purpureus

Hyacinth beans are great-value members of the pea family, with almost all parts of the plant edible and as much at home in the flower border as the veg patch. If you thought runner beans were vigorous, hyacinth beans easily outpace them, climbing up to 5m (16ft) in three months.

Quick guide

Sow indoors from early spring; outdoors once temperatures reach 18°C (64°F)

Ideal range 18-30°C (64-86°F), but tolerates higher

Grow in moist, well-drained soil in a sheltered, sunny spot

Water regularly during warm, dry periods, but avoid waterlogging

Reaches a height of 2-5m (6½-16ft), and spreads 1-2m (3-6ft)

Pick when pods are 5-10cm (2-4in) long

What is it?

The hyacinth bean is a short-lived perennial climber that is usually grown as an annual in cooler climates, but can be overwintered for replanting the following year. The young pods are a popular vegetable in India – think purple mangetout – and the dry mature seeds are also cooked and eaten, or used for seed sprouts. In Africa, the leaves are harvested too and cooked like spinach. Purple pods rival the sweet pea-like flowers for attractiveness, particularly those of 'Ruby Moon' with their deep burgundy tones.

Another name for the bean is "lablab", derived from the Arabic and thought to be an onomatopoeia for the rattle of seeds in the pods.

Hyacinth bean flowers are self-pollinating, which means just a single plant will provide a good crop of beans.

How do I grow it?

Originally from tropical India and China, hyacinth beans need warm temperatures to flourish. If the weather gets too cold, plants simply stop growing until conditions improve. In climates with cool winters and warm summers, extend the growing season by starting plants off indoors, and pot on until soil and air temperatures rise enough for planting outside. Where summers are cool, grow under glass in fairly large pots and, provided you maintain a humid atmosphere to prevent pest problems, you can look forward to a good harvest. As climbing beans, they will need some sort of vertical structure to romp over; tripods of bamboo canes are the classic choice.

The striking pods retain their colour if only briefly blanched in boiling water with a dash of lemon juice.

Step-by-step growing >>

Step-by-step growing

Hyacinth beans like warmth during germination. They will tolerate cooler conditions once established, but the best crops come from plants that have enjoyed consistent heat.

When to grow and harvest

Sow early for a long growing season and keep harvesting to encourage further flowering and cropping.

	early winter	late winter	early spring	late spring	early summer	late summer	early autumn	late autumn
sow			●	●				
plant out				●	●			
harvest					●	●	●	

1 Sow seeds

Soak seeds for 12 hours before sowing in small 9cm (3.5in) pots. Use moist potting compost and place 2 or 3 seeds in each pot, barely covering the seeds with compost. Place the pots on a windowsill or in a propagator at a temperature of 18–21°C (64–70°F). Thin out to leave only the strongest seedling.

Alternatively, if soil temperatures are warm enough, sow directly in their final growing position (see step 3).

Make multiple sowings at regular intervals for a longer harvest.

2 Harden off

Transplant seedlings into larger pots and continue growing at around 15°C (59°F) until outdoor temperatures warm sufficiently. So they don't suffer shock when planted out, harden off young plants for 2 weeks by placing them outside during the day and bringing them back in at night; or move them to a cold frame and open and close the lid.

Cold winds can damage young plants, so place them in a sheltered spot when hardening off.

3 Plant out

Transfer plants to a warm, sheltered, sunny position in moist, free-draining soil. Beans are hungry crops and it is worth enriching the soil by digging in well-rotted manure or compost. Set up climbing supports before planting and plant at the same depth as the compost in the pots.

15cm (6in)

15cm (6in)

Space plants at 15cm (6in) intervals and keep rows the same distance apart.

Growing in containers

min. 30cm (12in)

Grow in pots at least 30cm (12in) in diameter, filled with organic compost with added loam-based compost. If growing in a greenhouse, mist the air around plants and damp down the path by pouring water on it 3 times a day, if possible, to discourage red spider mite.

④ Aftercare, harvest, and winter care

Keep plants weed-free and, once established, feed every 2 weeks with high-potash tomato fertilizer. Water before the onset of dry weather to prevent the flowers dropping before they have had a chance to set. Harvest pods when they are still young and tender – no bigger than 10cm (4in) long – and pick continuously to encourage further flowering. Production will cease if pods are left unpicked, but if you have plants to spare it is worth leaving some to mature in order to harvest the seeds.

After autumn frosts have cut down the foliage, lift plants out by the root balls with a garden fork, being careful not to damage the roots. Store in a pot or tray of old compost for protection, in a cool, frost-free location, such as a garage or shed, for re-planting next year. Plants growing in warmer climates can remain outdoors all year round.

Tendrils may need tying in at first, but after that they will climb supports unaided.

Cook's tips

Keep fresh
Hyacinth beans do not store well: pick and eat the same day if possible.

How to eat
Prepare and eat young pods just as you would mangetout or green beans. Young leaves and shoots can be eaten, too.

- Lightly cook as a side vegetable: steam or boil for 1–3 minutes, or fry in a little oil with some chopped garlic.
- Add whole or sliced to stir-fries.
- For a quick-cook curry, make a tomato masala base, add the chopped beans with a little water, and simmer till tender.
- Mix raw or blanched into salads; they partner well with avocadoes.
- Slice and add to creamy pasta dishes: particularly good with pancetta or poached salmon.

How to preserve
Turn a glut of hyacinth beans into a bean chutney or piccalilli-style mustard pickle. Or leave excess pods to ripen fully then shell and dry the mature seeds on trays in a cool, airy place.

Quick guide

Sow under cover or direct at a minimum of 12°C (54°F)

Minimum -16°C (61°F) to maximum 32°C (90°F)

Grow in well-drained soil and full sun; avoid growing in clay

Drought-tolerant, but water as peas begin to swell to improve productivity

Plants grow up to 50cm (20in) in height

Pick immature pods like "petit pois" or ripe peas when they are large enough to eat

{ } **Level 2** *moderate*

Chickpeas

Cicer arietinum

To grow fully mature blond chickpeas, you need a long, hot growing season. But don't let that put you off as an equally tasty harvest can be had by popping open young, fresh pods for their bright green, immature peas. You can even snip off a portion of young shoots and leaves to be enjoyed in salads.

What is it?

Chickpeas are in the legume family of pod-forming plants that also includes peas, beans, and lentils. They produce relatively low-growing bushes with attractive, green foliage divided into paired leaflets, and bear flowers similar to those of a sweet pea. Like other legumes, they help improve soil fertility by taking nitrogen from the atmosphere through the action of bacteria that live in nodules in the roots. Because their root systems penetrate deep into the ground in search of water, they do not need vast amounts of watering for a successful crop.

Up to three peas can be found in a pod, and each pea sports a small beak-like protruberence, from which they get the name "chick-pea".

Chickpea flowers grow in varying shades of white, pink, purple, and blue, and usually start to bloom a couple of months after sowing.

How do I grow it?

Seedlings sown early indoors should be ready to plant out in rows after around 31 days, but first need to be acclimatized to outdoor conditions. They can also be sown directly from mid-spring. The large seeds do not need a fine seedbed and are happy in most soils, apart from clay. Improve very poor soils with well-rotted organic matter, but not too much as rich soil encourages leaves instead of flowers. Once growing, these drought-resistant, largely problem-free plants require little aftercare other than keeping down the competition from weeds.

Chickpeas can be picked when still green, and cooked and eaten whole like edamame.

Step-by-step growing »

Step-by-step growing

Chickpeas are a low-maintenance crop; just keep them free of weeds and water when the pods are swelling, or if the young plants appear stressed, to optimize your crop.

1 Sow indoors

Sow seeds indoors from early to mid-spring. Start by sprouting the seeds in a little water, then sow 4cm (1½in) deep in root trainers or 8cm (3in) pots filled with seed or multi-purpose compost, one seed per pot or trainer. Water well with tepid water and place the pots on a sunny windowsill or in a propagator set to a temperature of 12–25°C (54–77°F). Germination will take 7–10 days. Once sprouted, transplant them before the roots become congested, as the seedlings dislike root disturbance. Alternatively, if soil temperatures are warm enough, sow directly into the soil (see step 2).

Sprout chickpea seeds before sowing by leaving them for a day or so in shallow water or dampened kitchen towel.

2 Plant and sow outdoors

When the danger of frost has passed, harden off young plants for two weeks (see p.62) and, once acclimatized, plant them 7–15cm (2¾–6in) apart in rows 20–45cm (8–18in) from each other. Seeds can also be sown outdoors once the soil has warmed up, sowing directly into a level seedbed. Sow two seeds together, 5cm (2in) deep and 25cm (10in) apart. Water well until germination then remove the weakest plant of each pair, leaving the stronger seedling to grow.

Protect crops from birds with chicken wire.

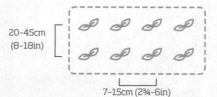

20–45cm (8–18in)

7–15cm (2¾–6in)

Space plants at the wider end of the range if growing in richer soil.

③ Aftercare

Once the young plants are established, chickpeas require little care other than weeding until a full leaf canopy has developed, which will then act as its own weed-suppressant. Remove weeds by hand or use a hoe, taking care not to damage or accidentally uproot the developing plants.

Plants growing in nutrient-rich soils will often put on leaf growth at the expense of flowers, and therefore peas. If your soil is particularly rich, you can counteract this tendency by feeding plants with a high-potash fertilizer to encourage flowering.

Plants produce a low, dense canopy of leaves that shades the ground and so discourages weeds from growing.

④ Harvest

Pick green pods regularly to encourage more cropping. Wear gloves to protect against the malic acid produced by leaves in hot weather, which gives them a red bloom and can be irritating to skin. Snap them or snip – either will do. If growing for the mature, blond peas, harvest when the pods are dry, preferably on a sunny day, but don't leave them too long on the plant or rodents may get at them.

After picking the mature peas, leave them on a tray to dry or use fresh.

Cook's tips

Keep fresh

Store chickpeas loosely packed in polythene bags in the fridge and use them as quickly as possible.

How to eat

Chickpeas are versatile. Eat them fresh, dried, whole, puréed, mashed, or ground.

- Steam green chickpeas and briefly sauté with garlic and chilli for a side dish.
- Sprinkle green chickpeas with smoked paprika and roast in the oven for a crunchy snack.
- Make a curry using chickpeas, Indian spices, kale, and grated fresh coconut.
- Combine cooked chickpeas with roughly chopped red onions, tomatoes, and parsley, then toss in a vinaigrette to make a delicious salad.
- Mix cooked chickpeas with Mexican spices, peppers, courgettes, and onions, then serve with tortillas, soured cream, guacamole, and lime wedges to make easy fajitas.

How to preserve

Cook until tender, cool, then dry. Once dried, refrigerate in a single layer in an airtight container for 3–4 days. You can freeze them for a year.

Level 2
moderate

Asparagus peas

Lotus tetragonolobus

If you love the taste of asparagus but don't have the time or space to grow it, this could be the perfect plant for you. While not the heaviest of croppers, what the asparagus pea lacks in volume it makes up for in the prettiness of its flowers and gourmet treat of its unusually finned pods.

What is it?

Asparagus peas are wildflowers of open fields and waste ground in their native Mediterranean habitat, and are thought to have spread further afield through imports of grain. Plants were first cultivated in gardens for their flowers, and it was only later that someone nibbled the pods and found they tasted delightfully of asparagus. Unlike many of their legume-family cousins, asparagus peas are trailing plants rather than climbers.

> The Latin name "tetragonolobus" means "with four wings" and refers to the arrangement of side fins on pods; when sliced they look like green stars.

The crimson flowers resemble those of broad beans and are similarly attractive to bees. The central "keel" petals are darker than the upright "banner" petals.

How do I grow it?

Seeds can be sown directly into the ground outdoors. As plants of the Mediterranean, however, they like warm soil to germinate and will need a little encouragement in cooler climates, either by first heating the soil with cloches or fleece, or by starting seedlings off under cover. Their attractive pea-like flowers make asparagus peas excellent "dual-purpose" plants for a mixed productive-ornamental border, or as a low hedge around the vegetable garden. The plants have a rather lax habit and if this isn't to your taste, try growing them through short pea sticks for support. If you pick pods regularly, plants will produce several harvests.

Pods are at their best when no larger than your thumb, and they should bend easily.

Step-by-step growing »

Step-by-step growing

If plants are left unsupported their spreading habit means you'll have few problems with weeds later in the season – they make productive ground cover under taller crops.

When to grow and harvest

Sow indoors for early harvests as plants are not frost hardy. Pick regularly to prolong cropping.

	early winter	late winter	early spring	late spring	early summer	late summer	early autumn	late autumn
sow indoors			●	●				
sow outdoors				●	●			
plant out				●	●			
harvest					●	●	●	

1 Sow indoors and plant out

In cooler climates or for earlier crops, sow seeds indoors at 19–21°C (66–70°F); germination can take up to 14 days. Sow in modules or 7.5cm (3in) pots of moist compost, two or three seeds to a pot, and thin to leave the strongest seedling. When 5cm (2in) tall, acclimatise plants to outdoor conditions (see p.32, step 2) before transplanting to rows at final spacings (see step 2). Water with liquid seaweed to help plants establish.

Pot on seedlings started in modules once they outgrow the space.

2 Sow directly outdoors

Sow seeds outdoors once the danger of frost has passed. Drills should be 2cm (¾in) deep and 38cm (15in) apart. Thin seedlings to 20–30cm (8–12in) apart along the rows, once large enough to handle. In cooler climates, sow under cloches or fleece to help warm the soil.

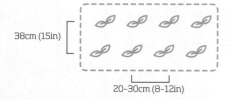

38cm (15in)

20–30cm (8–12in)

If you like neat rows, support plants with pea sticks or using garden twine tied to canes at each end of a row.

3 Aftercare

Birds, especially pigeons, can strip plants of leaves, so protect with netting if likely to be a problem. Water in dry spells, particularly when flowering and as pods develop; keeping the soil moist also avoids problems with powdery mildew. Feeding is not usually needed, but a high-potash tomato fertiliser will encourage flower and pod production on poor soils.

Keep young plants weed-free as they dislike competition when establishing.

④ Harvest

Pick pods regularly when they are 2.5cm (1in) long, checking your plants for the best-quality pods every day. It is worth doing so diligently as old pods become unpalatable, tough, and stringy. Harvesting is easier in the evening when the leaves close and pods are more visible.

Picks pods by pinching the ends between thumb and forefinger, or snip them off at the base with secateurs or scissors.

⑤ Cut back

Plants can start to lose energy later in the season and look a little worse for wear. To help prolong their vigour, cut them down to 10–15cm (4–6in) from the ground, using secateurs or garden shears, and this will usually stimulate a new flush of growth. Help them find their second wind by providing a few good soaks of liquid seaweed, and you should enjoy a sizeable late harvest. When plants finally die back, snip them off at the ground but leave the roots in the soil so they release all the nitrogen they've been fixing.

Cook's tips

Keep fresh

Best eaten as soon as possible after harvest, pods will keep in the salad drawer of the fridge for 2 to 3 days.

How to eat

Steam or lightly cook whole to preserve the subtle flavour, or slice finely into attractive crunchy "stars" that can be eaten raw.

- They are an excellent substitute for asparagus in most recipes, and perfect for fresh-flavoured stir-fries, either sliced or whole.

- Steam whole and toss in melted butter with a dash of lemon juice and some shredded mint, then eat on toast.

- Slice and add raw to a new potato salad with capers and chopped boiled eggs.

- Stir into mac'n'cheese before baking, either on their own or partnered with ham hock.

How to preserve

The pods can be pickled in lime juice or white wine vinegar, though you'll find they lose some of their delicate flavour.

SALAD VEGETABLES

Cucamelons are at their crunchy best when no more than 2–3cm (¾–1¼in) long.

{ Level 1 easy }

Cucamelons

Melothria scabra

Attractive and easy to grow, cucamelons pack the refreshing taste of cucumber with a zing of lime into one tiny, versatile fruit. They can be sliced and added to salads, pickled, cooked in stir-fries, dropped into cocktails, or blended into a cooling sorbet.

What is it?

This ancient crop has been enjoyed in Mexico and Central America since pre-Colombian times, but only in recent years has the rest of the world started to discover its delights. Don't be deceived by the daintiness of the stems, leaves, and fruit: it's a tough, drought-tolerant plant, and escapes the usual cucumber pests and diseases. Somewhat slow to get started, it is usually trained upwards, and will use its twining tendrils to climb and scramble rapidly up to 3.5m (11½ft). A single plant produces masses of fruit, so they are ideal for the smaller garden.

Cucamelons are known as sandía de raton *in Mexico, which means "watermelon for a mouse". Other monikers include "sour gherkin" and "pepquino".*

Cucamelon seeds need a warm, sunny windowsill or greenhouse propagator to germinate.

How do I grow it?

Cucamelons love the heat and will put on rapid, vigorous growth in warm, humid conditions, so you may want to grow them under cover in cooler climates. Bearing in mind the vigour of plants, you will need to provide them with a trellis, or lightweight arbour or obelisk, over which to scramble. Alternatively, they can be grown up a wigwam of canes like runner beans. Cucamelons are suitable for growing in hanging baskets or raised pots, although when scrambling over the ground they are less productive. After first raising from seed, plants are more fruitful grown on as perennials by lifting in autumn and planting out again the following spring.

Step-by-step growing

Cucamelons are happiest in a warm, sunny position with plenty of room to scramble or climb. Although they are fairly resistant to drought, regular watering is rewarded with prolific cropping.

When to grow and harvest

In cooler climates, the cropping season of cucamelons can be extended by starting plants off under cover.

	early winter	late winter	early spring	late spring	early summer	late summer	early autumn	late autumn
sow indoors		•	•					
sow outdoors				•	•			
plant out				•	•			
harvest					•	•	•	

① Sow indoors

Sow seeds under cover from late winter to early spring in seed trays, small pots, or modules of seed or multi-purpose compost, making sure the seeds sit vertically in the compost. Place them in a propagator or warm windowsill at around 20–24°C (68–75°F), where they will take up to four weeks to germinate. Once two or three seed leaves have developed, lower the temperature to 18–21°C (64–70°F). When seedlings are large enough to handle, transplant into 9cm (3½in) pots.

Transplant seedlings to larger pots so thay have space to grow.

② Transplant

After the risk of frost has passed, either harden off plants to acclimatize them to cooler conditions (see p.62) and transplant them to a sunny, sheltered location outside, or move them to a border within a warm greenhouse or polytunnel. Space plants at 15–40cm (6–16in) if growing in a border. Cucamelons can also be grown in containers, with two plants to a growing bag or one per large pot. You will need to provide climbing support: trellis, nylon netting, or sheep fencing is ideal. If using cane supports, older canes or hazel poles can be easier for the tendrils to grasp.

Tendrils find the ragged edges of older canes easier to climb.

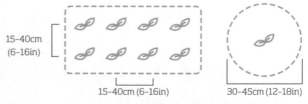

15–40cm (6–16in)

15–40cm (6–16in)

30–45cm (12–18in)

Grow in rows in a border, or plant singly in large pots, or two plants to a growing bag.

③ Aftercare

The stems may need tying to supports until the plants are established, especially if growing up canes. Once the main shoots reach 2.5m (8ft) pinch them out at their growing tips, and trim sideshoots back when they reach 30–40cm (12–16in) long. This will encourage bushier growth and direct the plant's energy to forming flowers and fruits rather than leafy growth. Water regularly and feed with a high-potash liquid fertilizer if needed to boost cropping. Cucamelons are very resistant to pests and don't tend to be troubled by diseases either, making them particularly easy to care for.

The climbing potential of cucamelons must be tamed by pinching out and pruning to encourage fruiting.

④ Harvest and winter care

Harvest begins after two or three months when the fruits are the size of small grapes. At the end of the growing season, but before the first frosts, lift the roots of plants and store them throughout the winter in a cool, frost-free place, covering the roots with coir or vermiculite and keeping them dry. Replant the roots the following year after the last frosts. Overwintered plants tend to crop earlier and more prolifically.

Cook's tips

Keep fresh
Store cucamelons in a sealed bag in the salad box of a fridge.

How to eat
Cucamelons can be eaten straight from the vine after washing and add a zesty freshness to salads, drinks, and preserves.

- Cut into halves or slice in salads or salsa.
- Toss simply with slices of pepper, olives, and a generous splash of olive oil.
- Use them in place of olives in a dry martini, or drop them into a gin and tonic or glass of Pimm's.
- Turn a glut into cucamelon chutney or pickle (see below).
- Partner with lime to make an unusual jam.

How to preserve
Cucamelons are perfect for pickling. Mix them with white wine vinegar, sugar, salt, and a mixture of fresh herbs such as dill, mint, or coriander. Boil until the sugar and salt dissolve, cool, and then refrigerate. The pickle will keep for 3–6 months in a sealed, sterile jar.

Achocha

Cyclanthera pedata

Level 2
moderate

This vigorous, easy-to-grow plant bears deep green, multi-lobed leaves and produces plump pods that taste of cucumber when soft and young, and sweet peppers when mature. Used as an anti-inflammatory, studies are also underway into its reputed ability to help lower cholesterol levels.

What is it?

Achocha is an extremely rampant climbing, scrambling vine native to Central and South America. In its natural habitat it grows at elevations of around 2,000m (6,500ft), where temperatures are cool but remain frost-free. So if you've always wanted to grow peppers, but don't have a warm enough climate, achocha makes an excellent alternative. Young fruits can be eaten raw in salads or as a snack, while mature fruits can be cooked. The shoots and young leaves are edible, too.

When to grow and harvest

Sow in spring for transplanting when the weather warms. Harvest through the summer and autumn.

	early winter	late winter	early spring	late spring	early summer	late summer	early autumn	late autumn
sow indoors			•	•				
plant out				•	•			
harvest						•	•	

If using bamboo canes for climbing support, they are best inserted at the same time as planting to avoid damaging the roots.

How do I grow it?

After sowing indoors, transplant outdoors, leaving it enough space to scramble over a trellis, frame, or netting. Pod production is best when the stems are supported, rather than grown over the ground. Grow in part shade in hot climates, to avoid sun scorch. Be warned: achocha is a rampant spreader and should only be grown under cover in areas with a short growing season.

① Sow indoors

Start seeds off in a greenhouse or sunny windowsill. Sow in late spring in small pots filled with rich seed compost, two seeds per pot. Place on a warm windowsill or in a propagator at around 20°C (68°F). Remove the weaker seedling after germination. When they look to be outgrowing their pots, transplant into larger ones.

Quick guide

Sow under cover and plant out once the danger of frost has passed

Minimum 8°C (46°F) to maximum 30°C (86°F)

Grow in rich soil in a warm, sheltered position, in sun or part shade

Water as required until established, depending on seasonal rainfall

Plants grow up to 3m (10ft) in both height and spread

Harvest continuously to encourage growth; pick young fruits and leave a few to mature

Cook's tips

Keep fresh
Fruits keep well for a week in a cool, dry place.

How to eat
Immature fruit can be eaten raw or pickled, but mature fruit is cooked. Leaves and young shoots can be eaten as cooked greens.

- Use as a substitute for cucumber in salads and dips.
- Snack on them filled with dill yoghurt.
- Stuff with a rice or meat filling and bake in a tomato sauce.
- Make savoury achocha jam.

How to preserve
Cut the ends off immature fruits and pickle in vinegar with sugar or mixed spices.

2 Initial care

Harden off after the last frosts (see p.62) and plant out around 1m (3ft) apart to give each plant enough space to flourish. Protect the soft stems from drying winds with fleece or a windbreak until established. Train the stems up a support as soon as possible to avoid them becoming tangled. Mulch with well-rotted organic matter once established. Feed with a general fertilizer, switching to a high-potash feed when fruits begin to form.

3 Aftercare and harvest

Achocha needs copious watering. Raise a circular ridge of soil 60cm (2ft) away from the base of the stem and about 7.5cm (3in) high. Fill this every time you water so it will soak down to the roots rather than draining away. Burying a flowerpot near the base of the plant, or cutting the bottom from a plastic bottle and burying it nozzle-down, has a similar effect. Harvest regularly to encourage pod production. Save seeds for next year, then compost after the first frosts.

{ } **Level 1** easy

Electric daisies

Acmella oleracea

Thrill-seeking gardeners take note! The tight, yellow, cone-shaped flowers of the electric daisy look bonny in a border, but when eaten, their mild citrus flavour is followed by a strong tingling sensation likened to popping candy, then numbing. The opportunities for creativity in the kitchen and surprising dinner guests are endless.

What is it?

The electric daisy is a bushy, trailing plant, with lush foliage and plentiful chrome-yellow flowers. Native to the warm climates of the tropics, it probably originates from Brazil, where it is known as *jambu* and its leaves are used to flavour salads and stews. The unusual properties of its flowers have long been known and are still used medicinally in many countries to ease the pain of toothache, mouth ulcers, and sore throats, giving rise to another of its names: "toothache plant".

The substance responsible for the flowers' electric effects also stimulates saliva production, so only sample a few at a time to avoid dribbling.

Keep plants in containers constantly moist and consider applying a ring of copper tape around the sides to deter adventurous climbing slugs.

How do I grow it?

Electric daisies are perennial plants in their native environment, but they are not frost hardy and, in areas where temperatures dip below 5°C (32°F) in winter, they are usually grown outdoors as annual bedding. Plants are easy enough to raise from seed each year, however, or they can be lifted in autumn and potted up for overwintering under cover, ready to plant out again next spring. The daisy-like flowers make a great addition to an ornamental border, provided plants are given enough space to pursue their trailing habit. They are also suitable for growing in large containers, which has the added benefit of affording some height protection against slugs.

Quick guide

Sow indoors from early spring or outdoors once risk of frost has passed

Grow in rich, moist soil in full sun or partial shade

Minimum 5°C (32°F) to maximum 35°C (95°F)

Water regularly and generously to avoid drought

Plants grow up to 40cm (16in) in height and spread

Harvest flowers and leaves from midsummer to autumn

The species bears plain yellow flowers, or there is a variety with red florets in the centre of the cone.

Step-by-step growing »

Step-by-step growing

These fast-growing, tender plants are easy to grow as annuals given a rich soil that is kept moist. Their colourful flowers suit ornamental borders and containers, as well as kitchen gardens.

When to grow and harvest
Start sowing indoors to prolong the growing season and pick flowers frequently to encourage more buds.

	early winter	late winter	early spring	late spring	early summer	late summer	early autumn	late autumn
sow indoors			●	●				
sow outdoors				●	●			
plant out				●	●			
harvest					●	●	●	●

1 Sow indoors

In cooler climates, sow seeds indoors at 20–24°C (68–75°F) in a propagator, on a warm windowsill, or in a greenhouse. Seeds need light to germinate and are best sown on the surface of trays of moist seed compost. They should germinate in 7–14 days. Once seedlings are about 5cm (2in) tall, carefully prick them out and plant individually into 7.5cm (3in) pots filled with multi-purpose compost. Continue to grow on under cover, repotting into larger pots if necessary.

Use a dibber to help prick out the tiny seedlings without damaging the roots.

2 Plant out

Once the risk of frost has passed, acclimatize plants by hardening them off for a week or so (see p.62). Improve soil fertility and structure at the planting site by digging in plenty of well-rotted organic matter. Leave the soil to settle for a few days, then plant your daisies with 35cm (14in) between plants and rows.

Seeds can also be sown directly into prepared soil outdoors after the last frosts. It can be helpful in cooler climates to warm soil with fleece or cloches before sowing. Sow several seeds at 35cm (14in) intervals and thin to leave the strongest.

Acclimatize young plants for a week or so before planting out.

35cm (14in)

35cm (14in)

Electric daisies are trailing plants and need ample room to spread.

③ Aftercare and harvest

Once established, plants will grow rapidly. Water often during dry weather and feed with a high-potash tomato fertilizer to promote flowering. Pinch out growing tips regularly to create bushy plants and maximise flowering. Protect lush young growth from slugs and snails. There are a variety of environmentally friendly ways to do this, such as encouraging predators like beetles and toads, using nematodes, dousing with garlic spray, and luring into hollowed-out grapefruits.

The flowers, buds, and leaves can all be eaten and, once plants are established, can be picked as required.

The electric effects of the flowers are best enjoyed in small doses, which means just a few plants are normally enough for one household.

④ Winter care and propagation

Plants will be killed by frosts, but it is possible to overwinter them by lifting in late autumn, potting up, and moving them into the house or heated greenhouse. Softwood cuttings taken during summer can be overwintered in the same way. To take a cutting, snip off a non-flowering shoot with two or three pairs of leaves and a 5cm (2in) stem. Remove the lowest pair of leaves and the soft tip of the shoot just above the growing point. Plant the cutting in a pot filled with moist cutting compost and place somewhere shady, ideally in a propagator.

Cook's tips

Keep fresh
Eat both leaves and flowers promptly after picking. They will keep for one or two days in the fridge.

How to eat
This plant's potent tingling effect means it is normally used raw, in small quantities, as a garnish or spice-like addition to dishes.

- In Brazil, the leaves and flowers are sliced and mixed with chillies and garlic in a traditional condiment eaten with chicken or fish.
- Chop and add raw flowers to salads for a splash of colour and buzzing flavour.
- Liven up cocktails by stirring in small amounts of shredded flowers, or to line the lip of a margarita glass.
- Cooked leaves have a more subtle flavour and make tasty leafy greens in spicy stews and soups.

How to preserve
Flowers hung up to dry after picking, and carefully stored away from moisture and light, will continue to produce their characteristic zap for at least a year.

Quick guide

Sow under cover in early spring, or outdoors when the soil has warmed up

Minimum -1°C (30°F) to maximum 30°C (86°F)

Grow in moist, light, free-draining, slightly acidic soil, in a sunny or partially shady spot

Water regularly but avoid waterlogging

Plants grow up to 60cm (24in) in both height and spread

Pick young, tender leaves, growing tips, and flowers from late spring to autumn

{ Level 1 easy }

Shiso

Perilla frutescens var. crispa

If you like basil then why not try growing shiso, its more spicy cousin with cinnamon-scented leaves? Popular in Japanese cuisine, shiso has soft, attractively wrinkled leaves in deep red and bright green varieties, which look impressive grown side-by-side in the herb garden.

What is it?

Shiso is native to China and is mentioned in ancient Chinese manuscripts. Brought to Japan in the eighth century, it was used in cooking and as a medicinal plant. In the West, shiso has mainly been grown for its ornamental foliage as a bedding plant, but more and more growers are discovering its culinary appeal. Both types are great in salads, as a wrap for sushi, or served with raw fish in sashimi; the green form is milder. The pretty, edible flowers can be used as a garnish, too.

When to grow and harvest

Shiso is a fast-growing crop, so harvest regularly when the leaves are young and tender.

	early winter	late winter	early spring	late spring	early summer	late summer	early autumn	late autumn
sow indoors		●	●					
sow outdoors				●	●			
plant out				●	●			
harvest				●	●	●	●	●

Plants in containers can be brought indoors before the first autumn frosts and kept in a cool, bright place as houseplants over winter.

How do I grow it?

Shiso is easy to grow but dislikes frost, so either buy plants from the garden centre after the last frost, or sow seeds in a heated propagator 8–12 weeks beforehand. Sow the seed fresh as it rapidly loses the ability to germinate. Shiso can withstand drought, but will give you a better harvest if you water it well. Grow it in window boxes by the kitchen for easy access.

① Sow indoors

Sow under cover in seed trays for planting out after the last frost. Sow seeds on the surface of moist, well-drained seed compost mixed with sharp sand to improve drainage, at a ratio of 9:1. Press lightly into the soil and cover with a little compost, perlite, or vermiculite. Cover the tray with newspaper and place on a shady windowsill or in a propagator at 22°C (72°F). Germination takes 15–30 days. Once sprouted, uncover and place in the sun.

Cook's tips

Keep fresh

Harvest in the morning. Place the leaves in a glass of water or keep sealed in a polythene bag in the fridge.

How to eat

Leaves, flower spikes, seeds, and seed sprouts can all be used to flavour or garnish.

- Try using shiso in any recipe calling for basil.
- Mix finely sliced leaves in Asian-style salads.
- Coat flowering shoots and leaves in batter and deep-fry.
- Mix leaves with grated radish and use to garnish a steak.

How to preserve

Freeze individual portions of chopped leaves in ice cubes.

② Pot on seedlings

Once the seedlings are large enough, carefully transplant them into individual pots. Repot seedlings each time they outgrow their previous pot, but before the compost gets too congested with roots and they become pot-bound. The final pot should be no larger than 9cm (3½in) as smaller plants establish better than large ones.

③ Plant out

Once all risk of frost has passed, harden off the young plants for a week or so by placing them outdoors during the day and bringing them in at night, or keeping them in a cold frame with the lid ajar during the day. Once the plants are acclimatized and the weather has warmed up, plant them out in rows, 30cm (12in) apart with 30cm (12in) between each row. Protect them with horticultural fleece or cloches at first, removing these once the weather is consistently warm.

{ Level 1 easy }

Rat-tail radish

Raphanus sativus var. caudatus

If you thought radishes were only about the roots, think again. While all radishes produce edible seed pods, the rat-tail radish doesn't focus on roots and instead puts most of its energy into producing a prolific number of spicy pods.

What is it?

Also known as the serpent radish, the rat-tail radish is an exotic variety of the humble garden radish, thought originally to have come from the island of Java in Indonesia and now popular throughout Southeast Asia. These annual plants can quickly grow to an impressive height, up to 1.5m (5ft) tall, bearing extensive, candelabra-like flowering stems from which the upright pods form. Pods are crunchy on the outside, juicy on the inside, and can extend to 30cm (12in) in length, but are best picked when still short and tender. The bee-friendly flowers are also edible and make a flavourful garnish, but don't pick them all or there'll be none to turn into pods.

Radish seed pods are a popular snack in Germany where they are traditionally enjoyed with beer – hence the variety 'München Bier'.

The small, delicate flowers can be pure white or tinged pink and will attract masses of pollinators into the garden.

How do I grow it?

Rat-tail radishes are fast-growing, cool weather plants that should still crop successfully sown early or late in the growing season. Sow direct and make repeat sowings as soon as the previous batch has germinated. Seeds can be sown in drills to form rows or broadcast and thinned out to the correct spacing. Don't try growing plants too close together as they resent overcrowding, and remove any encroaching weeds for the same reason. Keep well watered until they are established and continue watering regularly after that, to prevent the pods becoming tough. These tall-growing plants have relatively weak roots and will need staking to keep them upright.

Quick guide

Sow in succession from early spring until midsummer

Ideal range 10-16°C (50-61°F); germination fails above 35°C (95°F)

Grow in sun to part-shade, where soil has been manured for the previous crop

Keep the soil constantly moist

Plants grow up to 1.5m (5ft) high and 60cm (2ft) across

Pick when still young and tender; older pods turn hard and bitter

Step-by-step growing »

Rat-tail pods are pale green in colour, sometimes with pinkish markings, or there are purple-podded cultivars available.

Step-by-step growing

Rat-tail radishes need a constant supply of moisture to grow well, so plant them in deep, moisture-retentive soil, and give them plenty of room to grow. Plants are highly productive over a long period.

When to grow and harvest

Sow seeds under cover as early as late winter and outdoors until late summer, to extend the cropping season.

	early winter	late winter	early spring	late spring	early summer	late summer	early autumn	late autumn
sow indoors		•	•					
sow outdoors				•	•	•	•	
harvest				•	•	•	•	

1 Sow indoors

For an early harvest, begin sowing seeds under cover in late winter. Sow in modular trays, one seed per module – this will minimize root disturbance when the seedlings are lifted, whereas the roots of plants raised in trays can become intertwined, causing damage however gently they are teased apart. Pot on seedlings to individual pots when they have outgrown their modules, and plant outdoors in early spring at the final spacings given in step 2.

Heart-shaped seed leaves appear first, before the true leaves come through.

2 Sow outdoors

Sow seeds directly outside from early spring. Seed drills should be 1cm (½in) deep and 30cm (12in) distant. Sow evenly along the rows and thin seedlings to 20cm (8in) apart, or alternatively sow three seeds every 20cm (8in) and thin to leave the strongest seedling. You can also broadcast sow by scattering seed over the entire growing area and then thinning to the correct spacing. You will need to thin the seedlings out several times before the correct spacing is reached.

Thin out plants progressively, leaving the largest and strongest in place.

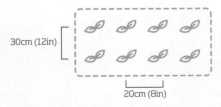

30cm (12in)

20cm (8in)

Avoid overcrowding by spacing rows 30cm (12in) apart and leaving 20cm (8in) between plants.

Each flowering stem can grow over 1m (3ft) tall and will produce numerous pods, as long as pollination is not interrupted.

❸ Aftercare

Keep the soil moist, but don't overwater them. Cover the developing plants with fine netting or horticultural fleece to protect them from cabbage white butterflies and their caterpillars, and flea beetles. If oilseed rape is grown nearby and has recently been harvested, you may find pollen beetle infestations can delay or hinder cropping. Oilseed is in the same family as rat-tail radishes and, after the crop has been harvested, the beetles turn to the radishes as a new food source, feasting on the flower pollen and thereby preventing pods from forming.

❹ Harvest

Pick the pods regularly when they are small to prolong the cropping season. Cut off the pods with scissors or snap them off with your finger and thumb. When plants die back at the end of the season, simply dig them out and add them to the compost pile.

Pods and plants are easily damaged, so take care when harvesting.

Cook's tips

Keep fresh
Wash pods and dry them thoroughly with kitchen towel, before placing them in airtight bags. Avoid overfilling the bags. They will stay fresh in the salad drawer of the fridge for up to one week.

How to eat
Radish pods add a crunchy texture and peppery flavour to raw or cooked dishes.

- Add raw to salads, whole or sliced depending on size.
- Cook briefly in stir-fries.
- Lightly steam or blanch and enjoy as a side dish.
- Add to curries and stews in place of okra.

How to preserve
Pickling is the best way to preserve the crunch and spiciness of the pods. Pickle them in white vinegar with sprigs of lemon verbena leaves, or in cider vinegar flavoured with smoked paprika. Leave for at least one month, or preferably longer, so that the pods have time to absorb the flavours.

Red orach

{ Level 1 easy }

Atriplex hortensis var. rubra

Adding splashes of natural colour can make any meal more exciting, and red orach leaves are some of the most vivid in the plant world. Pop in some succulent young leaves to brighten up a salad, and lightly cook mature leaves for a salty, purple alternative to spinach.

Quick guide

Sow under cover from early spring and outdoors from early summer

Minimum -30°C (-22°F) to maximum 35°C (95°F); leaves can scorch in hot sun

Plant in rich soil in a sunny or part-shaded position

Water freely for rapid growth

Plants reach up to 1.2m (4ft) and spread 30-60cm (12-24in)

Pick leaves as required throughout the growing season

Purple flowers are borne on flowering spikes and take the form of hundreds of papery disks, each enclosing a single seed.

What is it?

Red orach is a close relative of the common orach or spear saltbush *(Atriplex patula)*, a plant now thought of as a garden weed, but once considered a poor person's potherb. Red orach is the gourmet version, retaining all the vigour of a weed, but with a far more refined flavour. Plants grow tall and stand firm at over 1m (3ft) in height, and with the stems, spear-shaped leaves, and flowering spikes all displaying a deep red-purple hue, orach cuts a striking figure in the kitchen garden and would be a good choice for foliage colour in a mixed or ornamental context. Plantings work especially well alongside low-growing pot marigolds *(Calendula)*, whose edible orange flowers offer a striking colour contrast, both in the garden and side-by-side in salads.

How do I grow it?

Red orach is an annual that grows from seed each year, but this is the kind of plant you only need to buy once since it self-seeds so prolifically. In fact, it is highly advisable to pinch off the flower heads and collect the seed before it has ripened, or you and your garden risk becoming overwhelmed. Orach is fully hardy, but seeds need relative warmth to germinate, and for an early harvest it is best to start plants off under cover. Alternatively, sow directly outdoors once the soil has warmed up enough. For the largest, most succulent leaves, it pays to improve the soil with well-rotted organic matter.

Orach was once more popular than spinach and, with high levels of vitamin C and immunity-boosting ascorbic acid, used as a remedy for sore throats.

Repeat sow for a supply of smaller leaves, or sow two main crops a year and allow them to mature.

Step-by-step growing »

Step-by-step growing

Red orach is a hardy plant that can be harvested until late in the year. It needs a constant supply of moisture for optimum growth, so grow plants in moisture-retentive soil and water well in periods of drought.

When to grow and harvest
Make early sowings under cover for an early harvest, then direct sowings outdoors.

	early winter	late winter	early spring	late spring	early summer	late summer	early autumn	late autumn
sow indoors			●	●				
plant out				●				
sow outdoors					●	●	●	●
harvest				●	●	●	●	●

① Sow under cover

For an early crop, start sowing seeds under cover in early spring and you will have leaves ready to harvest by late spring. Sow seeds into modular trays filled with moistened potting compost and lightly cover the seeds with perlite (an inorganic compost additive) or fine layer of compost. Germination will take 7–10 days. Once sprouted, keep the seedlings well watered and transplant them to larger individual pots when they look to be outgrowing their modules.

Sow one seed per module and gently push out both seedling and compost to pot on.

② Harden off

Once all risk of frost has passed, harden off the young plants for a week or so by placing them outdoors during the day and returning them to shelter at night. Alternatively, transfer the plants to a cold frame, if you have one (it's a wooden box hinged at one end, with a tilted glass lid), and prop the lid open during the day before shutting it again at night. This allows the plants to become gradually accustomed to a harsher, more changeable environment.

Start hardening off on a mild day, gradually increasing the plants' exposure to colder temperatures, wind, and rain.

③ Transplant

Red orach can scorch in strong sunlight and is best grown in partial shade, or where plants will benefit from the shade of taller vegetables. Rich soil produces large, succulent leaves, so dig in plenty of well-rotted organic matter, if needed, before transplanting at the spacings shown in step 4.

4 Sow direct

Make further sowings directly outdoors to prolong the harvest. Sow every two or three weeks for a continuous supply of cut-and-come-again salad leaves, or for mature leaves sow a second crop in midsummer. Rake the soil to a fine tilth before sowing thinly in rows 12mm (½in) deep and 60cm (24in) apart. Cover lightly with soil and water with a fine rose on the watering can. Thin seedlings to 25cm (10in) apart.

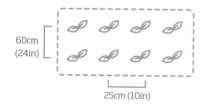

60cm (24in)

25cm (10in)

Leave 25cm (10in) between seedlings and transplanted plants, in rows 60cm (24in) apart.

5 Aftercare

Cover seedlings and young plants with netting to protect them from bird attack. Hoe regularly between rows to remove any weeds and keep the soil moist. Avoid splashing leaves if watering in sunshine, which can scorch them; watering in the evening is more effective and avoids the problem. Start harvesting the young leaves when the plant is around 10–15cm (4–6in) tall, leaving the mature leaves on the plant. For bushier growth you can pinch out the main stems and sideshoots by using your thumb and finger to remove the growing tips.

Tall, leggy plants may need to be supported by tying them to bamboo canes with garden twine.

Society garlic

Tulbaghia violacea

Level 1 *easy*

Society garlic is so-called because, though it tastes similar to garlic, eating it doesn't cause bad breath so you can chomp away on the leaves, stems, buds, and flowers with no fear of social offence. The flavour is actually more similar to wild garlic with a hint of pickled onion.

What is it?

This plant is from the African branch of the onion family and is more usually planted for ornamental bedding. Growing from rhizomes, plants produce neat clumps of flat, narrow leaves and bear clusters of fragrant, pale purple flowers on tall, slender stems. The flowering season is long, lasting from mid-spring to early autumn, and though blooms are few at the start of the season, numbers gradually increase towards the end.

Society garlic works well in containers as it is relatively drought tolerant and the flowers make it an attractive addition to a patio or balcony.

When to grow and harvest

Harvest leaves as required throughout the growing season and pick flowers and stems as they appear from midsummer.

	early winter	late winter	early spring	late spring	early summer	late summer	early autumn	late autumn
plant			•	•	•	•	•	
harvest			•	•	•	•	•	•

How do I grow it?

Tulbaghias make excellent plants for patio containers and are ideal for small gardens. Though not frost hardy, they will thrive in terracotta pots with a free-draining compost mix, and can be stored indoors in a cool, frost-free place over winter. They will also do well in a gravel garden, where the layer of gravel not only provides protection from light frosts in winter, but also stops them drying out too much in summer.

1 Plant out or in pots

Grow plants in a sheltered position in warm sunshine, in well-drained soil or, if planting in pots, gritty compost. Plant out container-raised plants any time from spring until autumn. Water the plants and allow to drain. Dig a hole slightly larger than the pot they are growing in and at the same depth. Water the base of the hole if the soil is dry and ease the plant carefully out of the pot, planting it at the same depth as it was in the pot.

② Aftercare and harvest

Plants in the ground need only occasional watering in dry conditions to maintain production of foliage and flowers. Water plants in containers every few days. Feed all plants with a high-potash plant food monthly, from mid-spring until early autumn. Pests and diseases are rarely a problem. Harvest leaves near the base to keep the plant looking neat. Picking leaves, buds, and flowers will encourage the plant to produce even more.

③ Winter care

Cut back stems to 3cm (1¼in) above the ground in late autumn. Society garlic doesn't tolerate cold conditions, so if you live in a cold area protect plants over winter with a 6cm (2½in) mulch of well-rotted compost. If you have planted them in a gravel garden then use straw or conifer clippings. Remove the mulch in spring when growth starts and the weather improves. Bring pot plants under cover.

LEAFY
GREENS

Ostrich ferns

{ 🍃 Level I easy }

Matteuccia struthiopteris

Do you have a dark, damp spot in your garden and don't know what to grow there? Plant a few of these shade-loving ferns and you'll be rewarded with an exquisitely beautiful green vegetable ready for picking in early spring when little else is available.

What is it?

Matteuccia struthiopteris is a deciduous fern, named for its resemblance to ostrich feathers. Its impressively large, bright green, infertile fronds emerge tightly coiled each spring from the crown, or rootstock, of the plant, and slowly unfurl. The coiled ends of these fronds are harvested for eating, and have a refined flavour between asparagus and French beans. Shorter, brownish fertile fronds appear later.

When to grow and harvest

The best time to harvest the tips is from early spring, before they unfurl.

	early winter	late winter	early spring	late spring	early summer	late summer	early autumn	late autumn
plant			•	•	•	•	•	
harvest			•	•				

How do I grow it?

Ostrich ferns dislike hot, dry summers and are perfect for growing outdoors in temperate regions. They look great planted in naturalistic groups and are happiest in a shaded area by a pond, but any sheltered, damp spot will do. Ostrich ferns spread by underground stems and it is not uncommon to discover new plants suddenly popping up quite a distance from the parent. They are best grown from young container-raised plants bought at a nursery or garden centre.

① Plant out

Thoroughly water the plants in their containers and allow to drain. Dig a hole slightly wider than their current pot, but at the same depth. Water the base of the hole if the soil is dry and allow it to soak away, then scatter a root-booster of mycorrhizal fungi over the base. Ease the fern gently from the pot, teasing out the roots, and position it in the hole. Firm the soil around the root ball to remove air pockets, and give it a good soak of water.

Plant ostrich ferns for the double benefit of an attractive plant and repeated cropping.

② Aftercare and harvest

Mulch around the plants with a 5–7.5cm (2–3in) layer of well-rotted compost to trap moisture. Ferns don't generally need feeding, but if plants are lacking vigour, apply a general-purpose plant food when they have just started into growth in spring. Let the ferns grow for a few years before harvesting, and harvest only up to half the frond or plants will not survive. Cut with scissors 3–5cm (1–3in) down the stem from the rolled fronds.

min. 40cm (16in)

Growing in containers

Grow singly in pots at least 40cm (16in) in diameter, in a mix of three parts multi-purpose compost, one-part sharp sand, and one-part John Innes No.3 or similar long-term compost. Feed with a general fertilizer during the growing season and keep the compost moist.

Quick guide

Plant young plants in early spring or autumn

Minimum -40°C (-40°F) to maximum 25°C (77°F)

Grow in a light to moderately shady spot in moisture-retentive, fertile soil or compost

Water frequently; never let the soil dry out

Plants grow up to 1m (3ft) with a spread of up to 50cm (20in)

Pick shoots early in the morning, before they unfurl

Level 1 easy

Sushi hosta

Hosta 'Sagae' and various species

Now's your chance to beat the slugs and snails at their own game and eat your hostas before they do. Try the tasty young shoots, stems, and leaves as a springtime delicacy in salads, stir-fries, sushi, or tempura. The edible flowers look pretty as a garnish, too.

What is it?

Hostas have been gathered from the wild for centuries in China and Japan, and are still popular in Japan where they are now grown commercially. Hostas are extremely hardy, shade-loving perennial plants normally grown in the ornamental border for their large, attractive, textured leaves. All hostas can be eaten, though traditionally the large-leaved species *Hosta montana* and *H. sieboldii*, and cultivar 'Sagae', are the plants of choice.

When to grow and harvest
Plant in spring or autumn and start harvesting when new shoots appear the following spring.

	early winter	late winter	early spring	late spring	early summer	late summer	early autumn	late autumn
plant			●	●			●	●
harvest			●	●				

Planting in spring allows a full growing season for the hostas to establish themselves, before you start to harvest the following year.

How do I grow it?

Hostas thrive in rich, damp soil and need plenty of moisture. All prefer a shady spot, though the tougher, large-leaved varieties can tolerate some heat; just avoid planting them in scorching sunshine. Hostas are great in small gardens as they do extremely well in containers, provided they are kept constantly moist and not left to outgrow their pots: when the existing container is full of roots, split them up and repot them.

Plant

Improve the soil with organic matter and leave to settle. Water the plant and allow the container to drain. Dig a hole slightly larger than the container and water the bottom. Once the water has drained away, scatter mycorrhizal fungi around the base of the hole where they will come into contact with the roots. Tease out the roots and plant the hosta so the compost surface is just below the level of the soil. Water thoroughly and mulch.

❷ Protect from slugs

If slugs and snails are a problem, consider growing them in pots where they are harder to access. There are numerous ways to provide protection: use environmentally friendly nematodes; encourage predators like ground beetles, frogs, toads, and thrushes; collect them by laying a sheet of hessian or plastic on the ground, or an upturned, hollowed-out grapefruit, then dispose of by hand; place copper tape round pots; or douse plants with garlic spray.

❸ Aftercare and harvest

Keep plants well watered during the growing season. Feed them with slow-release general fertilizer in spring to boost growth, but take care not to overfeed. When harvesting, take a few shoots from several plants rather than many from one plant, to encourage further growth. Remove and compost the leaves after they die back in the autumn.

Quick guide

Sow indoors from late winter, outdoors from mid-spring; autumn sowings possible

Minimum -20°C (-4°F) to 40°C (-104°F) or higher

Grow in full sun to part-shade, and keep crops weed-free

Water well, but they should survive a short dry spell

Grows up to 60cm (24in) tall with a spread of 45-60cm (18-24in)

Harvest young leaves for salads; pick berries when deep red and very ripe

Level 1 *easy*

Strawberry spinach

Chenopodium capitatum

You'd struggle to find a more "yin-yang" plant than strawberry spinach, which somehow combines a leafy green with a berry-bearing fruit bush in one quirky, eye-catching crop. Enjoy the young leaves raw in salads or lightly cooked, then stick around for the sweet delights of ripe red berries.

Tiny embryo fruits form at the leaf joints of the flowering stems. They are pale green at first, before taking on a pinkish tinge, then swelling to deep red.

What is it?

Native to northern USA and Canada, strawberry spinach is a hardy annual plant in the same family as beetroot and the edible weed fat hen. This helps explain why the roots, which are also edible, have a hint of the beets, and why you need to be careful not to mistake the seedlings for weeds. Plants form a low rosette of spear-shaped leaves with serrated edges, before sending out long flowering stems that form fruits along their entire length – which accounts for another of their common names: "strawberry sticks".

How do I grow it?

For the earliest crops, sow under cover from late winter, but take care to acclimatize the young plants to cooler conditions before planting out. Alternatively, direct sow after the last frosts, but be warned: germination outdoors can be erratic and take several weeks if the soil is not warm enough, so don't give up. Plants form a long tap root that makes them more heat-tolerant and drought-resistant than spinach, but for the most tender leaves and juiciest berries it is better to keep the soil constantly moist.

> The plant has spread around the world from North America, reaching Europe in the 1600s through exports of wool and birdseed.

The "strawberries" look much more like mulberries and are similarly composed of many small fruitlets.

Step-by-step growing »

Step-by-step growing

Strawberry spinach requires an open site on warm soil. Plants can be slow to get going if sown directly outdoors, and for the best chance of a bumper crop it pays to start seedlings off under cover.

When to grow and harvest

Sow indoors from late winter. Harvest young leaves from early summer and pick fruits when very ripe.

	early winter	late winter	early spring	late spring	early summer	late summer	early autumn	late autumn
sow indoors		●	●	●	●			
transplant				●	●			
sow outdoors				●	●			
harvest					●	●	●	

1 Sow indoors

For early crops, sow seeds under cover from late winter to early summer. Sow in pots, modules, or trays of seed compost, and cover the seeds with a light sprinkling of compost or vermiculite. Place in polythene bags on a sunny windowsill or heated propagator set to 15–20°C (59–68°F), and keep the compost moist. Germination should take around two weeks. When seedlings are large enough to handle, carefully transfer them to individual pots.

Grow on seedlings in cooler conditions but still under cover.

2 Transplant outdoors

Young plants should ideally still be quite small when planted out, to minimize root disturbance, but don't rush it as a frosty cold snap could kill them off. Acclimatize plants to outdoor conditions by placing them in a cloche or cold frame and gradually increasing ventilation, first during the day and then also at night. Carefully transplant them into their final positions at the spacings shown below.

Firm in the soil after planting and give the transplants a good soaking of water.

45cm (18in)

25cm (10in)

Plant in rows 45cm (18in) apart and leave 25cm (10in) between plants.

③ Sow outdoors

Strawberry spinach can also be sown directly outdoors, although germination can be slower if the soil has not warmed up enough and several sowings may be needed. Outdoor-sown seedlings also tend to grow more slowly at first. Sow seeds thinly in drills 1cm (½in) deep and 45cm (18in) apart, or scatter seed evenly over the seedbed and lightly rake in. Thin seedlings to 25cm (10in) apart when they are large enough to handle.

④ Aftercare and harvest

After transplanting, feed young plants with liquid seaweed until they are well established and remove any weeds that will otherwise compete for moisture and nutrients. Plants can tolerate a degree of drought, but it is best to keep the soil moist. Harvest a few leaves from several plants rather than stripping a large number from a single plant, which will then take time to recover. Berries are sweet enough to harvest when they are deep red and very ripe. Strawberry spinach is a prolific self-seeder and if you want to control seedling numbers it is best to remove all the fruits before they fall to the ground.

Berries are green at first and develop their rich red colouring as they ripen.

Cook's tips

Keep fresh
Both leaves and berries will keep for a week in the fridge. Place the leaves in a polythene bag and store the berries in a plastic container.

How to eat
The leaves can be used in place of conventional spinach in recipes. Young leaves are tender enough to be eaten raw, while mature leaves are better lightly cooked. The berries taste like nutty mulberries.

- Sauté the leaves with butter, garlic, and green beans for a tasty side dish.
- Top your breakfast muesli with a few berries for a sweet, musky flavour.
- Mix young leaves and berries with roasted baby beetroot and goat's cheese for a hearty, fruity salad.
- Try cooked leaves and berries as a topping for pizza with blue cheese.

How to preserve
Briefly blanch then quickly cool and dry the leaves before freezing. Berries are best eaten fresh but can be used to make a jewel-like jam with bite.

Cut leaves regularly and remove flowers; stems will re-sprout fresh growth from the base.

{ Level 1 easy }

Chrysanthemum greens

Chrysanthemum coronarium

If you thought chrysanths were only good for cut flowers, think again. The succulent leaves of the "crown daisy" species possess a sweetly herbal flavour and are robust enough to hold their shape well when added to stir-fries and stews.

What is it?

Originally from the Mediterranean, *Chrysanthemum coronarium* is now well established as an edible crop in China, Japan, and Vietnam, where it is grown almost exclusively for its leaves. In fact, the process of producing flowers causes a chemical change in the plant that turns the leaves tough and bitter. That said, however, it is still worth letting a few plants run to seed since the attractive, daisy-like flowers are themselves edible, and with even greater pungency than the leaves, a few scattered petals go a long way.

Look out for varieties described as having small or large leaves; the smaller-leaved types tend to have a stronger flavour.

Plants will grow quickly in a sunny position, but a degree of shade helps keep them cool in summer.

How do I grow it?

Chrysanthemum greens make a neat edging plant for the border or vegetable garden, and will also do well in containers for the patio or balcony. As fast-growing annual plants that can withstand a light frost, they are grown easily from seed – leaves can be ready to harvest just six weeks after sowing – and are ideal for climates with cooler summers, or for early and late sowings in spring and autumn. Plants actively dislike high temperatures, which can prompt them to produce flowers early, and it is best to avoid sowing seeds in spells of hot weather.

Quick guide

Sow outdoors every few weeks from spring until 10 weeks before autumn frosts

Minimum 4°C (39°F) to maximum 25°C (77°F), above which leaves turn bitter

Grow in sun or part-shade on any type of soil; growth is more tender in richer soils

Keep plants well watered

Can reach up to 50cm (20in) in both height and spread

Harvest the topmost shoots when about 20cm (8in) long

Step-by-step growing »

Step-by-step growing

Chrysanthemum greens are straightforward to grow and the secrets of success are simple: sow regularly, don't neglect the weeding, water regularly, and harvest often for tender leaves with the finest flavour.

When to grow and harvest
Chrysanthemum greens are productive over a long season, but keep harvesting to encourage young regrowth.

	early winter	late winter	early spring	late spring	early summer	late summer	early autumn	late autumn
sow indoors		•	•					
sow outdoors			•	•	•	•	•	
harvest			•	•	•	•	•	•

1 Sow seeds

For an early crop, sow seeds in modular trays under cover from late winter. Once all danger of frost has passed, harden off the seedlings (see p.62) to acclimatize them to outdoor conditions, then transplant into their final positions at the spacings indicated in step 2.

Once the weather is reliably frost free, sow seeds outdoors in drills or broadcast into a finely raked seedbed. To maintain a constant supply, sow every 3 weeks, sowing some in a sunny position and others in part shade; seeds in sunshine will germinate and grow faster than those in shade.

Seeds can be sown in succession from late spring to early autumn.

2 Thin out and protect

Thin outdoor-sown seedlings to 10cm (4in) apart. Thin successively to achieve the correct final spacing, always removing the weaker-looking seedlings. But don't let these weaklings go to waste: enjoy the thinned seedlings in salads or as a microgreen garnish. If the weather becomes unexpectedly cool early in the season, protect the seedbed or young growth with horticultural fleece or cloches.

Dampen the soil before thinning to make it easier to uproot seedlings.

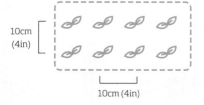

10cm (4in)

10cm (4in)

Sow or plant in rows 10cm (4in) apart and thin or space plants the same distance apart.

③ Aftercare and harvest

Keep plants free of weeds and well watered. Growth can turn lax and floppy once plants have matured and you may need to provide support with twine tied and wrapped around canes positioned at the ends of rows.

Plants are ready to harvest in 6–8 weeks, depending on the soil and growing conditions; growth is slower in cooler conditions and when temperatures are too high. Cut leaves while they are still firm, leaving some growth above the soil to allow for multiple harvests. If you do this, the plant can be cut several times and leaves will regrow. If you'd like to use the petal flowers as a garnish or in teas, leave a few plants and the ends of rows to grow on and produce flowers.

Watering regularly will promote tender growth and prevent plants running to flower at the expense of foliage.

Cook's tips

Keep fresh
Harvest in the morning when the weather is cool, put straight into a polythene bag, and store in the fridge.

How to eat
The taste of chrysanthemum greens is particularly suited to Asian cuisine, but it also goes well with the robust flavours of Indian and Mediterranean dishes.

- Chop and add to stir-fries.
- Steam, blanch, or lightly boil and add to stews at the last minute; overcooking turns the leaves bitter.
- Use young, mild leaves raw in a Korean-style salad with soybean paste and toasted sesame seeds.
- Scatter over a Taiwanese oyster omelette and allow the leaves to just wilt.
- Fry with garlic and add lemon and pine nuts for a side dish.

How to preserve
There are no worthwhile means of preserving the leaves, but the flowers can be dried and used in herbal teas.

Quick guide

Sow under cover in late spring or outdoors in summer

Minimum 5°C (41°F) but grows best at 20°C (68°F) or above

Grow in light, well-drained soil in a sunny, sheltered position

Water only in dry weather

Plants grow up to 1.2m (4ft) in height and 50cm (19in) in spread

Harvest leaves regularly during summer and autumn

Callaloo

Amaranthus leafy cultivars

{ Level 2 moderate }

Callaloo is an incredibly colourful leaf crop, closely related to the summer bedding plant love-lies-bleeding. Mature and baby leaves are packed full of vitamins and calcium and cooked like spinach, although they have their own distinctive earthy flavour.

What is it?

Callaloo is the name given both to amaranthus plants grown for their leaves and the Caribbean side dish cooked with them, but the leaves are also widely eaten in Asia, South America, and Africa. Amaranthus can also be grown to produce grain (see pp.136–9), and to avoid coarse leaves choose a cultivar selected for leaf quality, such as *Amaranthus* 'Red Army' or a cultivar of *A. tricolor*. Tender, heat-loving plants, they are grown as annuals in cooler climates and have an upright habit.

Callaloo flowers are smaller and more upright than the tassles of amaranthus grown for grains.

When to grow and harvest

Given heat, callaloo is a fast-growing crop. Regular picking is essential to keep tender new leaves coming.

	early winter	late winter	early spring	late spring	early summer	late summer	early autumn	late autumn
sow indoors				●	●			
sow outdoors					●	●		
plant out					●	●		
harvest						●	●	●

How do I grow it?

Callaloo grows best in temperatures above 20°C (68°F) and will not tolerate frost, so in temperate climates only a sheltered outdoor site will do. Delay sowing outdoors until summer, or start off indoors in late spring. Pot-raised plants are less vigorous, but can be planted out closer together to compensate.

1 Sow indoors

Sow early under cover to give these heat-lovers a head start. The tiny seeds are best mixed with sand to ease sowing. Sow 5mm (¼in) deep into large modules of well-drained, moist seed compost. Place in a propagator at 20°C (68°F) and cover to encourage germination in the dark; seedlings should emerge in 14 days. Harden off (see p.62) and transplant outdoors when large enough to handle and the temperature is above 16°C (61°F).

② Sow outdoors

Only sow outdoors when there is no longer a chance of frost. Warm the soil before sowing by covering with horticultural fleece for 2 weeks. Make drills 10cm (4in) apart for baby leaf crops or 30cm (12in) apart to grow more mature plants. Sow a seed and sand mixture at a depth of 5mm (¼in), then cover carefully with soil as well as fleece, if the weather is cool, to keep the soil temperature as high as possible. Germination may take upwards of 3 weeks.

③ Thin out and harvest

Thin outdoor seedlings to 13–18cm (5–7in) apart, giving the larger cultivars more space to spread. Pot-grown plants will not be as vigorous, so give them 10cm (4in) space in rows 25cm (10in) apart. Once watered in well and established, plants need little attention. Cut baby leaves when plants reach 10cm (4in) high, and more mature leaves as required. Remove the top rosette to encourage sideshoots and remove flowering shoots to maintain leaf growth.

{ Level 1 easy }

Walking-stick kale

Brassica oleracea var. longata

This crazy vegetable with a head for heights is a variety of kale native to the Channel Islands, where it has traditionally been grown to make walking sticks, as well as for food. The towering stems can reach up to 3m (10ft) in one season and the prolific top-knot of leaves provides an endless supply of superfood greens.

What is it?

Walking stick kale is a biennial that grows stems and leaves in its first year, before flowering the next. Part of the brassica family of cabbage-type plants, it faces stiff competition in the quirkiness stakes from cousins grown variously for mutant side buds (sprouts), monstrous flower heads (cauliflower), and Martian-like swollen stems (kohl rabi). In an 1836 volume of *The Farmers' Magazine* it was commented "these stupendous cabbages" are so nutritious they "will speedily produce the most surprising improvement in the growth... of cattle". And what is good for the cow is surely good for the gardener.

To make walking sticks, hang the stems for one year in a cool, well-ventilated place to dry out and harden, before sanding and varnishing.

Walking-stick kale is a very hardy plant and seedlings raised under cover do not need to be hardened off before they are transplanted outdoors.

How do I grow it?

Sow seeds under cover in early spring or outdoors in a seedbed for later transplanting. You will need to prep the soil a little before planting your seedlings: remove all weeds and make sure the soil is slightly alkaline by digging in lime if the pH is below 6.5. Growth is improved by adding well-rotted compost that is allowed to settle before planting, or where the soil has been improved for the previous crop, as the ground must be firm but not compacted. Net against cabbage white butterflies and pigeons, and support plants with stakes as they grow.

Sow in early spring for a late autumn harvest, or early summer to harvest the following year

Tolerates -15-30°C (5-86°F); grows best at 15-20°C (59-68°F)

Grow in a sheltered spot in sun or part-shade, in moisture-retentive, free-draining soil

Keep the soil moist for optimum growth

Usually reach 2-3m (6 ½-10ft) in height, with a spread of 60cm (24in)

Strip individual leaves, as needed, then finally the whole head and flowers

Step-by-step growing »

Provide supports for the stems and strip lower leaves to help plants grow straight and tall.

Step-by-step growing

Since walking-stick kale can grow to 3m (10ft) tall, plants need a spacious, open site and firm soil. Keep well watered at all times and net against pests for as long as possible.

When to grow and harvest

Sow in spring for transplanting, and harvest a few leaves from each plant as it grows.

	early winter	late winter	early spring	late spring	early summer	late summer	early autumn	late autumn
sow indoors			●	●	●			
transplant				●	●			
sow outdoors				●	●			
harvest						●	●	●

1 Sow indoors

To guard against clubroot, a common disease of brassicas, it is best to raise your own plants rather than buy in from unreliable sources. Sow seeds 2.5cm (1in) deep in modules filled with seed compost. Germination takes about 10 days. Before they start to outgrow the modules, pot on to individual pots filled with multi-purpose compost; don't allow seedlings to become pot-bound. Kale is extremely hardy and there is no need to acclimatize seedlings before planting out.

Take care when handling the seedlings as the roots are easily damaged.

2 Plant out

Seedlings should be ready to plant out 6 weeks after sowing. Water well and transplant to leave 80cm (32in) between plants and rows. Ensure the lowest leaf is touching the soil so the base of the stem is buried. Firm in the soil and water copiously to leave a puddle at the base of each plant. Alternatively, sow outdoors 7.5cm (3in) apart in a finely raked seedbed and thin to the same spacings. Fit cabbage collars round the base of stems to protect from cabbage root fly; these are discs 13cm (5in) in diameter with a slit cut to the centre and can be made of carpet underlay or similar.

Ensure the collar is flat on the ground to prevent the adult cabbage root fly laying its eggs at the base of the stem.

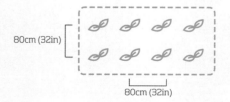

80cm (32in)

80cm (32in)

Leave plenty of space between plants so the huge leaves aren't restricted.

❸ Protection and aftercare

It is important to protect plants from the attentions of pigeons, which can strip young plants entirely, and of the caterpillars of cabbage butterflies and moths, which chomp many unsightly holes in leaves. Cover plants with horticultural fleece, or build a frame with stakes for fine mesh netting. Allow a gap between net and leaves so the adult insects cannot reach the leaves to lay their eggs. Keep plants weed free and well watered. Feed with a general fertilizer if growth looks sluggish, but do not overfeed as this makes the plants soft and the leaves prone to tearing. Stake and tie in plants as they grow.

Make sure the mesh of the net is fine enough to protect against small insects, such as cabbage white butterflies.

❹ Harvest and end-of-season

Harvest leaves as needed, stripping the lower leaves first and working up the stem to the canopy at the top. At the end of the growing season you have a choice: dig up and compost the plants; retain the stems and dry them out to fashion, Jersey-style, into walking sticks (they also make good plant supports); or leave these biennials to grow a second year, when they will produce flowers, which are edible and a source of nectar for bees.

Cook's tips

Keep fresh
Store the leaves in a sealed polythene bag in the fridge.

How to eat
Cook in the same way as ordinary kale and cabbage: chop and steam, boil, stir-fry, or braise. The flowers are also edible.

- Blitz up with fruit, coconut water, and spices for an energy-boosting smoothie.
- Roll whole leaves around a filling of rice and mince and bake in a tomato sauce.
- Pot-roast with game birds.
- Combine steamed leaves with fried pancetta, haricot beans, and cream, sprinkle with breadcrumbs and cheese, and bake for a hearty gratin.
- Stir shredded leaves into soups, stews, or curries for the last 5 minutes of cooking.
- Pick the flowers and scatter in salads.

How to preserve
Rinse leaves and pat dry with kitchen paper, then freeze in bags for up to 2 months. Shredded leaves can also be salted and fermented for sauerkraut.

Quick guide

Sow under cover in early spring or outdoors once soil has warmed

Ideal range 10-30°C (50-86°F) or more; good crop for hot climates

Grow in full sun or part-shade in any well-drained soil

Keep plants well watered

Plants grow up to 1m (3ft) high and spread to 45cm (18in)

Harvest leaves when young and pick flower heads just before the flowers open

{ Level 1 easy }

Huauzontle

Chenopodium nuttalliae

This productive, unfussy crop tastes like broccoli and is far easier to grow. No wonder it is such a popular vegetable in Mexico, where locals snack on cheesy fritters made from the unopened flowers. The name is pronounced "wow-zon-telay", but you could just call it Aztec broccoli.

What is it?

This member of the Goosefoot family of plants, which includes red orach, amaranth, and beetroot, can grow into large bushes 1m (3ft) or more tall and wide. It is believed to share the same parentage as quinoa, another crop in the *Chenopodium* genus, but was used for its leaves and shoots rather than seeds, and was developed in the hot, dry regions of Mexico to grow among the corn stems. As they mature, plants undergo an intriguing colour change from green to yellow and pink.

When to grow and harvest

Sow seeds early and plants will be mature enough for harvesting at the beginning of summer.

	early winter	late winter	early spring	late spring	early summer	late summer	early autumn	late autumn
sow indoors			●	●	●			
sow outdoors				●	●	●	●	
plant out				●	●			
harvest					●	●	●	●

Huauzontle grows quickly and its unopened flower heads and leaves can be harvested in as little as 7 weeks after sowing.

How do I grow it?

Huauzontle is easily grown from seed and will flourish in hot weather, making it an ideal crop for warmer climates. Plants are productive even in poorer soils, but more prolific if you enrich the planting site by digging in plenty of organic matter. Be warned: seedlings are almost identical to the weed fat hen, so be careful not to pull them out by mistake!

1 Sow seeds

Sow indoors from early spring in modules. Given warm conditions, seeds should germinate in just 3 or 4 days. Once all risk of frost has passed, harden off seedlings (see p.62) and plant outdoors with 30cm (12in) distance between plants and rows. Handle carefully and try to avoid root disturbance. You can also sow directly outside on to a finely raked seedbed; sow more than you need and thin to 30cm (12in) between plants.

Keep fresh

Flower heads, leaves, and shoots will store for a couple of days in a polythene bag in the fridge.

How to eat

Steam or blanch in boiling water; all parts hold their texture well.

- Make traditional Mexican fritters: mix grated cheese and eggs with cooked huauzontle, form into patties, and fry till golden. Serve with a tomato or chilli sauce.

- Add fresh to stir-fries, curries, and stews.

How to preserve

All parts can be blanched, quickly cooled, and frozen.

② Aftercare

Give plants a feed of liquid seaweed and keep them well watered until established. Protect from pigeons with horticultural fleece or netting when the plants are small. Slugs and snails may also be a problem: try using organic controls such as garlic sprays, beer traps, and nematodes, and encourage natural predators (ground beetles, toads, etc.). Plants may need supporting on windy sites with stakes or canes.

③ Harvest

Harvest the tiny flower heads before they open, and gather leaves from the top 10cm (4in) of each flowering stem, picking a few leaves from each plant to avoid a check in growth. Plants quickly produce more side stems for further harvests. Pick the leaves before they start to turn a deep red colour, after which they take on a bitter taste. Young shoots can also be eaten.

Quick guide

Sow from late spring, or earlier under cover; early to mid-autumn sowings can succeed

Minimum 18°C (64°F) to maximum 30°C (86°F)

Grow in moist, humus-rich soil in a sheltered, sunny spot

Water well before the onset of a drought; keep soil moist but not waterlogged

Plants grow up to 30cm (12in) in height and 20cm (8in) in spread

Harvest when leaves are 2.5-10cm (1-4in) long

Level 2 moderate

Salsola

Salsola soda, S. komarovii

Bring the flavours of the foraged seashore to your garden with one of the best-kept culinary secrets of Italy and Japan. The succulent leaves of salsola have a crisp bite and salty tang that make it an excellent alternative to samphire and seaweed.

What is it?

Plants in the genus *Salsola* are found growing throughout Asia, North Africa, and the Mediterranean. In Italy, *Salsola soda*, commonly called "agretti", is a regional delicacy sold fresh in the markets of Umbria and Lazio, while in Japan, the lower-growing *S. komarovii* or "okahijiki" is immensely popular. Also known as "land seaweed" or "saltwort", these are short-leaved, salt-tolerant plants that grow in grassy clumps, like chives. Plants are found on coastal salt marshes in the wild, but you don't need to live by the sea to cultivate it at home.

When to grow and harvest

Sow early and pick the young shoots or leave to mature before harvesting from late spring.

	early winter	late winter	early spring	late spring	early summer	late summer	early autumn	late autumn
sow indoors			•	•	•			
sow outdoors				•	•	•	•	
plant out				•	•			
harvest				•	•	•	•	•

After sowing indoors you can transplant seedlings outdoors, but only when any risk of frost has passed.

How do I grow it?

Salsola tolerates poor soil, but prefers alkaline conditions and needs warmth to germinate and sunlight to flourish. Plants are best raised from seed, but the germination rate is notoriously low. Buy fresh seed, sow plenty, and be ready to sow as soon as the seed arrives.

1 Sow indoors

Although not a heat-loving plant, seeds need warm temperatures to germinate and are best started off under cover in a heated propagator set to 23–26°C (73–79°F). Sow seeds 5mm (¼in) deep in pots or modules filled with compost. Seeds tend to germinate in 7 to 10 days, but occasionally take a little longer. Repot seedlings in larger pots, as needed.

2 Plant out or grow outdoors

Transplant indoor-raised seedlings to their growing area outdoors, spacing them 15cm (6in) apart. Further crops can be sown directly outdoors if the soil is warm enough for germination. Rake a level seedbed and sow 5mm (¼in) deep in rows 10cm (4in) apart, or broadcast the seed. When the seedlings have developed a few sets of leaves, thin them to 15cm (6in) apart; you can eat the thinnings!

3 Aftercare and harvest

Remove any weeds and keep plants well watered for the plumpest leaves; watering with slightly salted water is not essential, but it does make a difference to the taste. Feed with a general fertilizer to boost growth only if needed. Leaves can be harvested as a cut-and-come-again crop by shearing off the tops to encourage plenty of young, tender regrowth. Stop harvesting when plants begin to flower.

ROOTS, BULBS, AND SHOOTS

Quick guide

Start off under cover in spring for planting out after the last frosts

Minimum 0°C (32°F) to maximum 30°C (86°F)

Will crop in poor soil but prefers deep, rich soil; needs a sunny, sheltered spot

Drought-tolerant, but water well in dry spells to ensure large tubers

Grows up to 2.5m (8ft) high and spreads up to 1m (3ft)

Lift tubers after the first frosts

Level 2 moderate

Yacón
Smallanthus sonchifolius

If you like the texture of water chestnuts and the taste of watermelon and pear, then try growing yacón. Sweet, crisp, crunchy, and juicy, the delicious tubers well deserve their alternative name of Peruvian ground apple, and can be eaten raw as a snack, roasted, or added to stir-fries.

Usually grown as a perennial for its tubers, yacón can also be grown as an annual plant and harvested for its edible young main stems.

What is it?

Yacón has been cultivated as a crop in South America for 2,000 years and can be found growing in the Andes up to elevations of 3,000m (9,843ft). The root system of each plant is made up of large, plump tubers, which are dug up for eating, and smaller knobbly roots, which can be stored over winter and replanted the following spring. The sweetness in the tubers comes from a type of sugar called inulin, which is not easily broken down by the body. This means you can enjoy a sweet hit without the calories, but may end up feeling a little gassy...

How do I grow it?

Yacón will thrive in most soils where there is reasonable rainfall and a good amount of sunlight, but they do need plenty of space to spread out, making them unsuitable for growing in pots. Although a long growing season is required for a decent harvest, unlike many South American root crops the plants do not need short days before forming tubers and so can be grown more easily in northerly latitudes. You need to position them in a sunny area, however, as the heat-to-light ratio must be correct: too much heat and too little light means leggy plants. Yacón is a distant relative of the sunflower and, with its huge fuzzy leaves and attractive yellow flowers, looks good in the flower border or the veg patch.

In Spanish colonial times, yacón tubers became a staple food for sailors, who found they stored extremely well over the long transatlantic crossings.

The flesh of the tubers ranges in colour from white through pale yellow and orange to purple.

Step-by-step growing »

Step-by-step growing

Yacón should be grown in moist, well-drained soil rich in organic matter. In temperate zones this plant bursts into growth after the summer solstice, and from then on has an increased requirement for water.

When to grow and harvest

Start tubers into growth in early spring and harvest when the foliage is blackened after the first frosts.

	early winter	late winter	early spring	late spring	early summer	late summer	early autumn	late autumn
plant indoors			●	●				
plant out				●	●			
harvest							●	●

1 Plant indoors

Start plants off under cover in early spring. Fill 15cm (6in) pots with rich compost and plant a tuber in each pot just below the surface. Place in a greenhouse at around 20°C (68°F), or on a warm windowsill. A combination of too much heat and too little light causes the stems to become leggy; such plants will never thrive, so balance the ratio of light to heat by placing the plants in a bright area.

The first shoots may be yellow, white, or even colourless, but this is quite normal and tubers will soon put on leafy growth.

2 Plant out

Transplant the tubers into larger pots if necessary. Acclimatize the young plants to the colder temperatures outside by placing them in a cloche or cold frame and gradually increasing ventilation, first during the day and then also at night.

When the soil is warm and there is no further risk of frost, plant them in their final positions, leaving about 90cm (3ft) between plants and the same distance between rows. Yacón is a hungry crop and will benefit from having well-rotted manure or other organic matter dug into the soil before planting.

Give the young plants a good soak both before and after planting.

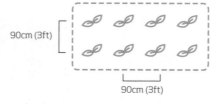

90cm (3ft)

90cm (3ft)

Plants ultimately put on lots of tall, leafy growth and need to be spaced well apart.

③ Aftercare

Protect young plants from late frosts and cold snaps with cloches or horticultural fleece. Once established, these resilient plants aren't much bothered by pests or diseases, but you may need to pick off slugs and snails from lower leaves.

Yacón grows slowly at first and it's worth planting a quick catch-crop of radishes, spinach, or lettuce in the space around them, not least to help suppress weeds. Keep plants thoroughly watered once they go into overdrive in midsummer. Yacón stems can reach a height of over 2m (6½ft) and on windy sites plants may need to be given some support.

Provide support by tying plants individually to canes or stakes, or by running string around stakes positioned at the perimeter of the planting area.

④ Harvest and propagation

Once the first frosts have blackened the foliage, lift the plants carefully to avoid damaging the tubers. You will find two sets of tubers: the large storage tubers, which are for eating, and above them in the crown of the plant are the smaller rooting tubers from which you can propagate next year's crop. After removing the large tubers, cut back the stems to about 7.5cm (3in), transfer each crown to a box or large pot of moistened compost, and store over winter in a cool but frost-free place under cover. New shoots will start to appear next spring and, when they do, cut out each tuber with its shoot, ready for the next crop.

Propagate next year's crop from the small tubers at the top.

Quick guide

Plant bulbs in early autumn in their final flowering positions

Minimum -1°C (30°F) to maximum 25°C (77°F)

Grow in clay or moist, free-draining soil in sun or part-shade; prefers a dry rest

Keep moist during the growing season in spring, but can dry out in summer

Plants grow up to 1.25m (4ft) in height and 80cm (32in) in spread

Dig up bulbs when the stems die down in summer, or all year round after flowering

---

{ Level 1 easy }

Camas

Camassia quamash

Camas bulbs were once an important wild harvest for first nation peoples in North America, who would bake them *en masse* in fire pits. Be warned: they are the ultimate slow-food vegetable, taking anything from 12 to 48 hours to cook – but the sublime taste is worth the effort.

What is it?

Native across much of western Canada and northwestern USA, camas is a long-lived perennial bulb, coming back year after year to produce spectacular, dense spikes of vivid blue, starry flowers in late spring. Establish a large clump in the garden, then you can lift some to eat when they die down and replant the others. Bake overnight or steam in a slow-cooker until the pale bulbs have turned a deep chestnut brown. After cooking, they taste somewhere between baked figs, roasted chestnuts, and caramelized onions.

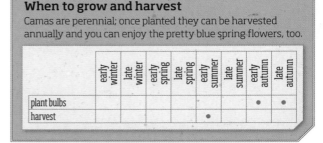

When to grow and harvest

Camas are perennial; once planted they can be harvested annually and you can enjoy the pretty blue spring flowers, too.

	early winter	late winter	early spring	late spring	early summer	late summer	early autumn	late autumn
plant bulbs							●	●
harvest					●			

How do I grow it?

In its native habitat, camas is found in wet prairies and meadows that often dry out by late spring. Aim to replicate that environment in the garden with humus-rich soil that retains moisture but is not waterlogged in winter. If you experience a dry spring, water the plants until the foliage dies down.

Harvest bulbs that are 2.5–5cm (1–2in) in diameter in early summer, after the flowers have died back.

1 Prepare the soil

If necessary, improve the soil before planting to make it more moisture-retentive and free-draining. Incorporate well-rotted organic matter, such as homemade compost or soil conditioner from the garden centre, forking it into the soil surface or taking the opportunity to dig over the ground. If the soil is sandy, mulching annually with a thick layer of well-rotted compost is essential, too.

2 Plant bulbs

Buy plump, healthy, undamaged bulbs for autumn planting. Scatter bulbs randomly for a natural effect, planting them where they fall. Plant 8–20cm (3–8in) deep, twice the depth of the bulb and the same distance apart. Camas can also be grown in large, deep pots of moisture-retentive compost, with a layer of drainage material at the base. Protect the pots from frost in a garden shed, garage, at the base of a sheltered wall, or under a hedge – but don't forget about them!

3 Aftercare

Water plants in the ground in spring if dry. For pot-grown camas, start watering in spring to encourage growth and keep pots well watered, but allow them to dry out once the leaves have died back, mimicking what happens in nature. Feed camas in pots in spring and after flowering with high-potash fertilizer. Protect bulbs over winter with a thick layer of mulch on the soil surface, and move pot-grown plants to a cool but sheltered site under cover.

Tubers come in a range of shapes and sizes, from knobbly to rounded to long and slender.

{ Level 2 moderate }

Dahlia yam

Dahlia cultivars

What, eat a dahlia? Yes you can! The petals of the flowers can be added to salads as a colourful garnish, and the sweet, starchy, nutty-tasting tubers can be peeled and enjoyed raw or cooked. Just be sure to save a few large tubers for planting again next spring.

What is it?

Dahlias are perennial plants that grow from tubers to produce a vibrant summer display of large, colourful flowers, before dying back in autumn ready to sprout again in the spring. Native to Mexico and Central America, dahlias were first grown by the Aztecs for their sweet-potato-like tubers and Spanish Conquistadors brought them back to Europe in the 16th century as an edible root crop. The Victorians decided such showstoppers were better suited to the flower border than the veg patch, and that's where they stayed – until now!

The Aztecs of ancient Mexico used the dried hollow stems of "tree dahlias" (Dahlia imperialis) as pipes for plumbing and irrigation.

Dahlia '**Black Jack**' bears dark crimson semi-cactus blooms and produces tubers with red skins and smooth flesh.

How do I grow it?

First you need to pick the right variety, as there are hundreds available and some are tastier than others. Cactus-flowered varieties are generally a good bet, producing the mightiest tubers as well as the largest flowers; "DeliDahlia" cultivars have been developed especially for eating. If growing in an ornamental border, be aware that a fair proportion of blooms must be removed if you want to enjoy a sizeable harvest of tubers. In milder areas, tubers can be left in the ground to overwinter, but in regions where the ground becomes frozen in winter they will need to be lifted and stored under cover.

Quick guide

Plant out tubers after the last frosts; bring stored plants into growth in late winter

Minimum -5°C (23°F) to maximum 25°C (77°F)

Grow in a sunny spot in organic-rich, free-draining soil

Tubers have a high water content and need lots of watering

Plants can reach 1m (3ft) high and spread 40cm (16in)

Harvest tubers in autumn when the foliage is blackened by the first frost

Step-by-step growing »

Step-by-step growing

Dahlias are sold in most garden centres, so should be easy to find. They need rich soil, a sheltered site, and the support of a stake. Provide plenty of water throughout the growing season, but do not overfeed.

When to grow and harvest
Dahlias need a long growing season: plant in late spring and harvest in autumn

	early winter	late winter	early spring	late spring	early summer	late summer	early autumn	late autumn
plant out				•	•			
harvest							•	•

1 Prepare your plants

When the dahlia crowns sprout shoots 2-3cm (¾-1¼in) high in spring, divide them into smaller clusters of tubers or individual sections, ensuring each section has roots and shoots. You can then either plant out immediately, if your climate is warm enough (see step 2), or pot up in separate containers filled with compost and grow on under cover until risk of frost has passed.

Alternatively, take cuttings of the new shoots of sprouted tubers when they are 5-7.5cm (2-3in) long, retaining a small piece of tuber. Trim the leaves from the base of each cutting, dip in rooting powder, and plant in a free-draining compost. Keep at 21°C (70°F) until they root, then pot on individually into 9cm (3½in) pots filled with compost. Plants grown from cuttings are usually stronger and healthier.

2 Plant out

A few weeks before planting, incorporate plenty of well-rotted organic matter into the soil and allow to settle. At the same time, if you have grown on plants under cover, harden them off to outdoor conditions (see p.62). To plant, push a stake or cane into the ground to provide a support for each dahlia as it grows. Leave a space of 90-120cm (3-4ft) between plants. Dig a hole at the base of each support 10-15cm (4-6in) deep and slightly larger than the section or cluster of tubers. Backfill with soil and firm in, leaving a slight saucer-shaped depression to hold water.

Position the tubers or young plants so they are right up against the support.

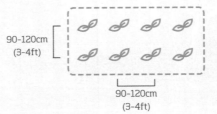

90-120cm (3-4ft)

90-120cm (3-4ft)

Space plants at 90-120cm (3-4ft) intervals in rows the same distance apart.

❸ Aftercare

Keep plants well watered: the ground should be constantly moist. Dahlias also need protection from slugs and snails and there are a variety of environmentally friendly ways: encourage predators like ground beetles, frogs, toads, and thrushes; use nematodes; lay a sheet of hessian or plastic on the ground, or an upturned, hollowed-out grapefruit, then collect and dispose of them by hand; or douse plants with garlic spray.

Start feeding with high-potash fertilizer when you notice that the flower buds are beginning to develop. Leave some buds to bloom but nip out the majority, as the plants' energies are better spent increasing the size of the tubers.

Dahlia flowers are too pretty to sacrifice entirely, but most should be nipped in the bud.

❹ Lift and store

Once the first frosts have blackened the foliage, cut stems back to within 5cm (2in) of the base and carefully lift the tubers. Move any clusters not being using immediately to a dry, cool, frost-free location. To discourage rot, turn the clusters upside down for a few weeks so water drains from the hollow stems. Retain one cluster of each variety from which to propagate next season's crop.

Store an entire cluster of tubers from each variety. These can then be divided and planted out, or grown on under cover, when shoots emerge the following spring.

Cook's tips

Keep fresh
Store the tubers as you would potatoes, in a cool, dark, dry place.

How to eat
The tubers can be eaten either raw or cooked. The edible flowers are also tasty as a garnish or chopped up in salads.

- Peel, cube, steam till tender, then mash with lots of butter.
- Toss with oil, honey, and rosemary and roast with other root veg or on their own.
- Grate and combine with egg, flour, chopped onions, and herbs to form cakes, then shallow-fry till golden.
- Cut into very thin slices, then fry or oven-bake to make sweet-tasting crisps.
- Make a winter-warming soup enriched with cream and spiced with cinnamon.

How to preserve
Blemish-free tubers store for long periods in a cool, dark, airy place. Do not store where dry air encourages desiccation. Check regularly and eat any showing the first signs of shrivelling.

No need to peel
mashua tubers before cooking: the skin is nutty, nutritious, and not at all tough.

Mashua

Level 1 *easy*

Tropaeolum tuberosum

With long twining stems, attractive grey-green leaves, and showy flowers, mashua will look wonderful in the veg patch climbing over a trellis. Eaten raw the tubers have a peppery, aniseed flavour, which becomes milder when cooked. The leaves and flowers are also edible and make a great addition to salads.

What is it?

A close relative of the garden nasturtium *Tropaeolum majus*, mashua is a bushy, scrambling plant native to the Andes mountains in South America, where they have long been valued as a crop for their ease of cultivation, resistance to disease, and ability to be left in the ground and harvested as needed. The tubers are the size of small potatoes and vary in colour from cream to purple-striped. Outside of South America, mashua is more usually grown as an ornamental garden plant, with cultivar 'Ken Aslet' a popular choice.

Mashua was used in traditional medicine to suppress the libido and Inca emperors fed it to their armies "that they should forget their wives".

Cultivar 'Ken Aslet' bears attractive orange flowers with long red spurs.

How do I grow it?

Mashua flourishes in warm rather than scorching hot summers and needs a long growing season, since the tubers of most varieties only start to form when the period of daylight is 12 hours or less. The cultivar 'Ken Aslet', however, will form tubers regardless of the length of daylight. Mashua is suitable for growing up netting, wire fencing, or an upright column, but they don't climb well on a tripod of canes unless you wrap string around it. Alternatively, allow them to scramble over the ground. They can also be grown in large pots or barrels of moisture-retentive compost.

Quick guide

Plant out tubers once the danger of frost has passed.

Minimum 4°C (39°F) to maximum 20°C (68°F)

Grow in moist, rich, well-drained soil in a sheltered sunny or partially shady spot

Water well during the growing season or they will go dormant

Plants climb up to 2.5–4m (8–12ft) and spread up to 1m (3ft)

Cut back foliage after the first frost and lift the tubers

Step-by-step growing »

Step-by-step growing

Start tubers into growth under cover in cooler climates. Plant outdoors in rich soil and keep it constantly moist. Mashua will tolerate a part-shaded position as it doesn't like to get too hot in summer.

When to grow and harvest

Mashua is a long-season crop: plant in spring and harvest when the stems are cut back by autumn frosts.

	early winter	late winter	early spring	late spring	early summer	late summer	early autumn	late autumn
plant indoors			●	●				
plant out				●	●			
harvest							●	●

1 Plant indoors

Start mashua off in early spring by planting tubers 3cm (1¼in) deep in individual pots filled with moist compost. Place somewhere warm and bright and keep the compost moistened. Meanwhile, clear weeds and stones from the planting ground outdoors and, 2 or 3 weeks before planting, dig in plenty of well-rotted organic matter to improve nutrition and drainage. Allow to settle.

Mice love to eat the tubers and you will need to provide protection, such as a glass or plastic barrier, if growing in a greenhouse.

2 Plant out

Once the danger of frost has passed, plant out the young plants with 30cm (12in) space all round, and water in well. You can also plant tubers directly outdoors at the same time, 3cm (1¼in) deep and 30cm (12in) apart. Plants can be slow to emerge, especially in colder areas, and it's worth covering with cloches or horticultural fleece to encourage growth. Also consider raising a crop of fast-growing vegetables like spinach, lettuce, or radish in the space between plants, harvesting before the mashua sprouts.

A thick mulch of well-rotted organic matter will help boost growth, retain moisture, and cool the roots.

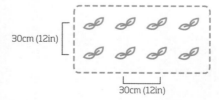

30cm (12in)

30cm (12in)

Leave 30cm (12in) between young plants and tubers, and the same distance between rows.

③ Aftercare

Protect young plants from slugs and snails by one or more environmentally friendly methods, such as dousing with garlic spray, using nematodes, and laying organic traps. Keep the area weed free until plants are established, when the foliage of these vigorous scrambling plants will act as a weed-suppressant. Provide plants with climbing support, such as netting, rings of fencing wire, hazel sticks, or canes. Water constantly to plump up the tubers; plants go dormant if the soil dries out for long periods.

Mashua will happily scramble over free-standing circular supports, or can be trained up canes and sticks.

④ Harvest

Lift tubers in autumn after the first frosts. Clean the soil from the tubers and make sure they are dry, before storing in a cool, dry, frost-free place. Retain some medium-sized tubers for planting the following year, but exclude those of plants affected by mosaic virus, which manifests as a patterned mottling on leaves.

Lift plants carefully and eat any damaged tubers as soon as possible.

Cook's tips

Keep fresh
Store somewhere cool and dark, but not in the fridge.

How to eat
Eaten raw and straight out of the ground or storage, the tubers are pleasantly spicy, but if cooked or left in a sunny spot for a week or so, they develop a much sweeter taste. Leaves and flowers can also be eaten.

- Slice raw tubers and eat them like radishes in salads.
- Add leaves and flowers to salads for the same spicy kick as watercress and rocket.
- Cook tubers as you would potatoes: boiled, mashed, sautéed, or roasted.
- Fry parboiled cubes in butter with bacon and shallots, stir in a handful of the leaves, and pour over beaten egg for an Andean frittata.

How to preserve
Blemish-free tubers store for long periods in a cool, dark, airy place. Check regularly and eat any with signs of shrivelling. Do not store where dry air causes desiccation, or where light and warmth may start the tubers into growth.

Chinese artichoke

Level 1 easy

Stachys affinis

Easy to grow and similar in flavour to the Jerusalem artichoke, but without the hugely tall growth and (ahem) associated digestive issues, the Chinese artichoke is well worth a try, especially in smaller gardens. And don't let the odd, segmented appearance of the plump, little grub-like tubers put you off.

What is it?

A perennial member of the mint family, Chinese artichoke is native to wet ground in regions of China, but is cultivated for its creamy-coloured tubers all over eastern Asia. The tubers are also popular in French cooking, where they are called *crosnes*, and the plant is gradually becoming more widely known in the West. Attractive mounds of slightly furry, mint-like foliage make it a handsome addition to a veg patch or decorative border.

The purple flowers are a magnet for bees in summer, but are often pinched out to divert the plant's energy towards the tubers.

When to grow and harvest

Plant tubers at any time while dormant. The new harvest will not be ready until late autumn.

	early winter	late winter	early spring	late spring	early summer	late summer	early autumn	late autumn
plant outdoors	•							•
earth up stems					•			
harvest	•	•						•

How do I grow it?

Given good soil in full sun, the Chinese artichoke is trouble-free to grow. Tubers can be planted outdoors at any time while dormant, as long as the soil is not frozen. Plants start into growth early, when temperatures reach 5°C (41°F), and grow quickly in moisture-retentive soils to provide good ground cover.

 ## 1 Plant outdoors

Work plenty of well-rotted compost into the soil before planting. Plant dormant tubers from late autumn till early spring. Place them with their points upwards, about 8cm (3in) deep and 30cm (12in) apart, leaving 45cm (18in) between rows. Cover with soil and wait for shoots to emerge in spring. Alternatively, tubers can be started into growth under cover in pots filled with moist compost and planted out when their shoots are 10cm (4in) long.

Cook's tips

Keep fresh
The thin-skinned tubers quickly discolour in light, so leave them in the ground and dig up as required; they remain in good condition through frosts and snow.

How to eat
Enjoy raw or cooked like Jerusalem artichokes. The tubers don't need peeling.

- Lightly steam before using in stir-fries like water chestnuts, or frying in butter and garlic.
- Slice thinly, mix with kale, and bake with cream for a gratin.

How to preserve
In Japan, they are pickled with shiso (see p.54), which dyes the tubers red, and eaten at New Year.

② Aftercare

Protect the new shoots from slugs and snails and keep plants well-watered at all stages of growth. On light soils, apply a thick mulch of compost in early spring to help retain moisture. Earth up the stems in summer when they reach about 30cm (12in) tall to initiate the growth of as many tubers as possible. Pretty as they are, you should pinch out most of the flowers to concentrate the plant's energy into tuber formation, but try to leave a few for the bees!

③ Harvest

Chinese artichokes can be harvested at any time from late autumn until they begin sprouting in early spring, but they taste sweeter once there has been a frost on the ground. Cut the plant's top growth back as it dies away in late autumn and simply unearth tubers as required. In cold areas, mulch with the old stems to help keep the soil workable. Leaving a few tubers in the soil after harvest will produce new plants to supply the following year's crop.

Oca

Oxalis tuberosa

Level 2 *moderate*

This fascinating root crop is a delicious alternative to potatoes, producing good yields of colourful tubers that are about the size of baby new potatoes. Unlike potatoes, oca is not affected by blight, but it can struggle to crop well in cold climates, as the plant is frost tender and the tubers don't develop until late autumn.

What is it?

Oca originates from the central Andean region of South America, where it has been widely cultivated for centuries and remains an important crop. The plant was also introduced to New Zealand in the 19th century, where it has become a popular staple and is known as New Zealand yam. Numerous cultivars are available, which produce tubers with different coloured skins from white through to purple. All types can be eaten raw or cooked, and the crisp flesh has a slightly sharp sour-apple tang, which is more pronounced in some varieties than others.

> The tubers' sharp taste comes from oxalates in their skin, chemical compounds that can be reduced by leaving them in sunlight before eating.

Oca is an attractive crop with bright yellow flowers and lush foliage consisting of large, clover-shaped leaves.

How do I grow it?

Oca is a tender perennial which, like potatoes, is grown as an annual crop, although its preferred longer, frost-free growing season can be a challenge in cooler regions. Before planting the tubers, first encourage them to start sprouting by placing them in a light, cool, but frost-free place (the same process as chitting potatoes). Once chitted, either plant the tubers in rows directly outdoors when the risk of frost has passed, or give them a head start by planting in pots to begin growth indoors. Once in the ground, oca plants need little attention aside from earthing up to encourage tuber formation, which is initiated by the shortening lengths of the days in autumn. Don't unearth the tubers until the foliage has been cut back by frost. If the frosts arrive too early, the plant may die and not grow any tubers, so listen to the weather forecast and cover with horticultural fleece if needed.

Oca tubers come in various colours, depending on cultivar, including pink, purple, yellow, and white.

Quick guide

Plant indoors in early spring, or outdoors once the risk of frost has passed

Minimum 4°C (39°F) to ideally 20°C (68°F), but tolerates higher

Grow in well-drained soil in full sun

Water during dry spells, especially as tubers form in autumn

Plants grow up to 50cm (20in) high and 30cm (12in) wide

Harvest in early winter when foliage has been frosted

Step-by-step growing »

Step-by-step growing

Wider spacing allows these bushy plants to produce higher yields of tubers and to spread by rooting their stems into the soil. Don't worry though, oca is not invasive like some other members of the *Oxalis* genus.

When to grow and harvest

If you have a short growing season between spring and autumn frosts, get a head start by planting tubers indoors.

	early winter	late winter	early spring	late spring	early summer	late summer	early autumn	late autumn
plant indoors			●	●				
plant out				●	●			
earth up						●	●	
harvest	●	●						

① Plant indoors

Tubers start sprouting from mid- to late winter. When they do, space them out on a tray in sunlight to chit and slow further growth. If left in the dark they produce long, fragile shoots that break on planting. In cooler climates with a risk of spring frosts, plant each tuber about 8cm (3in) deep in moistened multi-purpose compost in a 15cm (6in) pot. Grow on in the greenhouse or on a sunny windowsill.

Store tubers in a cool, frost-free place and check for signs of growth.

② Plant out

When all risk of frost has passed, if planting tubers directly outdoors, make drills about 8cm (3in) deep and 90cm (36in) apart. Then plant the tubers along the drills, spacing them 45cm (18in) apart. Gently rake soil back over the drills and then cover with a layer of fleece to help warm the soil.

If you have started plants off under cover, harden off the young plants to the colder temperatures outside by placing them in a cloche or cold frame and gradually increasing ventilation, first during the day and then also at night. Plant out at the same spacings.

A string guideline and batten with measurements marked on are useful tools when planting in rows.

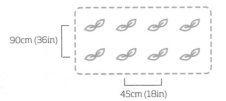

90cm (36in)

45cm (18in)

Wide spacing allows these bushy plants to produce higher yields of tubers.

❸ Aftercare

Protect young plants with horticultural fleece while they establish, and also later if unseasonal frost is forecast. Mulch around the plants with well-rotted compost in summer to help retain moisture in the soil; a moist growing medium is essential for the promotion of tuber development.

In late summer and early autumn the plants should be earthed up in the same way as potato crops, by drawing soil up around the base of the plants. This encourages stem rooting and the development of further tubers. Water during dry spells, especially in autumn, when the tubers start to swell in response to shortening day length.

The trefoil-shaped leaves can also be picked and eaten in salads, but don't harvest too many or you will reduce the plants' ability to form tubers.

Carefully uncover the tubers with a fork or by hand and save a few for planting next spring.

❹ Harvest

The longer the plants stay in the ground the better. If early autumn frosts are predicted it is worth covering them with cloches or fleece to extend the growing season. Once foliage is blackened by frost, leave to die back completely for at least 2 weeks before harvesting the tubers. The sharp flavour of the flesh can be reduced by exposing tubers to sunlight for several days.

Taro corms are a type of modified underground stem and form just below the soil surface.

Taro

Level 3 advanced

Colocasia esculenta

Unless you live in a tropical climate, cultivating taros for their sweet-potato-like corms can be a struggle. Gardeners in cooler climates need not despair, however, as they can still be grown for their beautiful "elephant ear" leaves, which are deliciously edible in their own right.

What is it?

Taro is a perennial rainforest plant that evolved its large, slightly concave, heart-shaped leaves to help shed water from tropical downpours. The sweet, starchy corms are an important staple root crop in Southeast Asia and southern West Africa, and taro cultivation has a central place in Hawaiian culture. In the Caribbean, taro is mainly grown for its leaves, and is often used as the main ingredient in the vegetable stew "callaloo".

Taro has a claim to being one of the oldest food crops in the world, with evidence of cultivation dating back some 7,000 years.

The species has fresh green leaves and stems, but you can also buy cultivars with black stems and purple leaves.

How do I grow it?

For corm cultivation, taros need long, hot summers, moderate to high humidity, and plenty of water; in the tropics they are usually grown in boggy ground. In cooler climates, plants can be grown in a warm greenhouse for their edible leaves and are regularly successful outdoors, too. They grow in a range of soils from clay to deep, rich loam, and in small gardens can be grown in large containers of rich, moist compost. The easiest way to obtain corms for planting is to buy them from an Asian, West African, or Caribbean grocery shop. Otherwise, cultivars selected primarily for their ornamental foliage can be purchased from specialist nurseries.

Step-by-step growing »

Step-by-step growing

Taro is a tropical crop so growth is faster in warm, humid conditions. In cooler climates, grow in a greenhouse or polytunnel, or as container plants for a sunny patio or a warm, bright spot in the house.

When to grow and harvest

Start into growth in early spring. Harvest young leaves in summer and the corms in autumn.

	early winter	late winter	early spring	late spring	early summer	late summer	early autumn	late autumn
break dormancy			●					
plant on				●				
harvest					●	●	●	

1 Plant corms

Start plants off under cover in early spring by planting corms in individual pots of moist compost. Place the pots in a warm greenhouse, or preferably in a propagator set to a temperature of around 30°C (86°F), or as warm as possible. Once the corm dormancy is broken, a new growing shoot will poke through the compost. Keep at a high temperature until the first set of leaf shoots emerge.

Taro corms have an obvious growing tip, and should be planted with the tip uppermost and only just covered by compost.

2 Transplant

Move the pots out of the heat and grow on under cover, transferring to larger pots as they grow. Keep well watered using tepid water; a good trick is to stand the watering can in the greenhouse to warm for 24 hours before use.

Where temperatures remain above 15°C (59°F) throughout the growing season, young plants can be planted outdoors in late spring. Prepare the site by digging in plenty of organic matter and allow to settle. Remove any weeds before planting and rake the soil to a rough level. Plants can also be moved to a growing bed in a warm greenhouse.

Move plants out of the heat needed to break dormancy once they show a pair of leaf shoots, but continue to grow under cover.

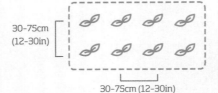

30-75cm (12-30in)

30-75cm (12-30in)

Space plants 30cm (12in) apart in warm but temperate climates, or 75cm (30in) apart if your climate is hot and humid.

③ Growing in pots

Taro plants can be grown outdoors in summer in cooler climates by potting them on into large containers. Fill the containers with a 50:50 mix of multi-purpose and loam-based composts, and place them in a warm, sheltered, sunny location.

Taros can also be grown as houseplants, primarily for a harvest of edible leaves, in a warm bathroom, office, or conservatory. Mist plants with tepid water regularly where the air is dry, or stand on a tray of pebbles filled with water. Grouping taro with other houseplants increases the humidity around the plant.

The large, heart-shaped leaves evolved to cope with tropical downpours and make taros appealingly architectural plants for pots.

④ Aftercare and harvest

However you grow your taros, keep them constantly moist, always watering with tepid water. Feed weekly with a liquid general fertilizer and also with a high-potash fertilizer 2 or 3 times per season.

Harvest young leaves as required, but not too many from a single plant. Withhold water before harvesting corms so the leaves die down. Lift when needed and store in a cool, dark place with good ventilation.

Level 2 moderate

Yam bean

Pachyrhizus erosus

There is something slightly odd about sowing a bean to produce a root crop but, as all parts of the plant above ground are toxic, only the delicious crisp white flesh of the yam bean tuber makes a suitable food crop. In fact, the seed pods contain the chemical rotenone, which is used as an insecticide.

What is it?

The yam bean is a perennial climber native to Mexico and is widely cultivated as an annual crop in Central America and Asia. It has many names over this range, including Mexican turnip, jícama, and singkama. In these subtropical and tropical climates, the vigorous vine can grow to 5m (16ft) high, with blue or white flowers like sweet peas, followed by flat pods and huge tubers. More modest crops are possible in temperate climates with a frost-free growing season of 5 months.

When to grow and harvest

Sow these tender plants early indoors and harvest as late as possible in autumn.

	early winter	late winter	early spring	late spring	early summer	late summer	early autumn	late autumn
sow indoors			•					
plant out				•	•			
harvest							•	•

Start plants off under cover in spring to provide a long enough growing season.

How do I grow it?

Sow indoors, then plant outdoors or grow on in large containers in a greenhouse. Support the sprawling vines which, pruned to about 1.5m (5ft) high, make an attractive, fast-growing screen. Remove flowers to maximize tuber size.

① Sow indoors

Sow seed indoors 6 to 8 weeks before spring frosts are expected to finish. Soak in water for about 12 hours before planting to soften the seed coat and speed up germination. Sow in 7.5cm (3in) pots of moist compost, 5cm (2in) deep, and place on a warm windowsill or in a propagator at 20–23°C (68–73°F). Grow on until the last frost has passed. If roots peep through the bottom of the pots before this, transfer plants to larger pots.

2 Plant on

Prepare soil by digging in well-rotted compost and covering
with fleece to raise the temperature. Put cane supports in
place. Harden plants off by moving them outdoors during the
day and under cover at night, for 2 weeks. Space plants 20cm
(8in) apart, leaving at least 60cm (24in) between rows. If
growing in a greenhouse, transplant to a border or move each
plant into a large pot, with a diameter of at least 38cm (15in),
filled with rich, multi-purpose compost.

3 Aftercare and harvest

Usually free of pests and diseases in temperate regions, yam
bean grows rapidly in warm weather. Water outdoor plants
generously in dry spells, and those in pots daily. Apply liquid
tomato fertilizer weekly once flowering begins, and remove
blooms and pinch out tips when they reach 1–1.5m (3–5ft) to
encourage tuber formation. Tuber growth is linked to short
days, so harvest as late as possible before the frost, covering
with fleece on cold nights, if needed.

{ } **Level 1** easy

Earth chestnut

Bunium bulbocastanum

A truly multi-purpose plant, the underground tubers, leaves, and seeds of the earth chestnut are all edible. While yields of the tubers may be modest, the rosettes of finely divided leaves and foamy clusters of white flowers are easily pretty enough to grace both productive and ornamental borders.

Delicate, white, lacy flowers start to bloom in early summer. The seeds are sometimes known as black cumin and can be harvested.

What is it?

Bunium bulbocastanum is a relatively small, hardy, perennial plant found growing in grassland throughout western and southern Europe, and is from the same family of plants as carrots and parsley. As its common name suggests, the flavour of the cooked tubers is similar to chestnut, while the raw leaves are akin to parsley, and the seeds taste like a smokier version of cumin. With such a variety of culinary delights in one plant, the earth chestnut deserves to be far more widely cultivated. It shares a common name (and the name pignut), with the similar, but larger, *Conopodium majus*, which is also edible, so check the Latin name to avoid confusion.

How do I grow it?

Seeds can be sown directly into the soil outdoors, but germination is more reliable when sown under cover. Young plants should then be grown on in pots and planted out once dormant in autumn. Harvesting of leaves and seeds can begin in the second year, but the small tubers are slow to swell, making it best to begin harvesting them only at the end of the third growing season. In addition, plants often produce smaller baby tubers, which can be eaten or planted in autumn and grown on. In the wild, earth chestnuts grow in chalky meadows and therefore do well in gardens with alkaline soil.

The species name "bulbocastanum" gives away what's beneath the soil: a swollen root (bulbo) with the flavour of sweet chestnuts (castanum).

Tubers are crisp and refreshing raw, turning sweet and chestnut-like when cooked.

Quick guide

Sow under cover from early spring, or outdoors from late spring

Minimum -15°C (5°F) to maximum 30°C (86°F)

Grow in sun or partial shade in moist, well-drained soil

Water after planting, then only in very dry weather

Reaches a height of 60cm (24in) and a spread of 25cm (10in)

Harvest tubers from autumn, leaves from spring, and seeds from late summer

Step-by-step growing >>

Step-by-step growing

Earth chestnuts are tough plants that are easy to grow, but to harvest tubers you need to dig up entire specimens and this means new plants must be propagated each year from seed or surplus tubers.

When to grow and harvest
Sow in spring and grow on in pots before planting out when dormant in autumn. Harvest from the second year.

	early winter	late winter	early spring	late spring	early summer	late summer	early autumn	late autumn
sow indoors			●	●				
sow outdoors				●				
plant out								●
harvest tubers	●	●						●
harvest leaves				●	●	●	●	

Give seed-raised plants a full growing season in pots before planting out in autumn.

① Sow seeds

In spring, sow seeds thinly in seed trays, cover with a thin layer of compost, water well, and place in a cold frame or greenhouse. Germination is usually within 14 days. Once the seedlings are large enough to handle, carefully prick them out individually into small pots. Continue growing them in their pots for the first summer, either in the cold frame or outdoors, keeping the compost moist but not waterlogged and transferring to larger pots as needed. Plant out, at least 30cm (12in) apart, once the leaves have died down in autumn.

Seeds can be sown straight into the soil, but germination tends to be more erratic than those sown under cover. Where rows are required, sow generously into drills about 38cm (15in) apart. If the aim is a more natural drift of plants, scatter seed over the planting area. Either way, thin seedlings to 30cm (12in) apart when large enough to handle.

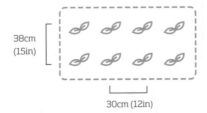

38cm (15in)

30cm (12in)

Whether in rows or drifts, space plants at intervals of 30cm (12in).

2 Aftercare and harvest

Earth chestnuts rarely succumb to pest problems and are resilient plants, but if you want the tubers to swell as much as possible ensure plants are kept watered during dry spells of weather. Plants are hardy and need no winter protection.

Only begin harvesting from the second year of growth. Leaves can be picked sparingly from late spring into autumn, bearing in mind that it's the leaves that feed the swelling tubers. Seed should ripen by late summer, when the whole heads can be cut and dried. Tubers are best lifted with a fork when the plants are dormant, from late autumn through winter.

The leaves look and taste similar to flat-leaf parsley, but don't pick so many that the tubers suffer.

Propagate new plants by dividing a large, established clump into smaller sections.

3 Propagate

As harvesting the underground tubers requires lifting the whole plant, more will need to be planted for the supply to continue. Fortunately earth chestnuts are easy to propagate and you have a choice of methods. New plants can be raised from seed in spring, using seed saved the previous summer. Any tubers that are too small for eating can also be planted in pots in spring and grown on for a season. Or if you leave a few plants to mature and bulk out, these can be lifted in spring or autumn and carefully divided into several smaller plants, then replanted.

Cook's tips

Keep fresh
Eat leaves promptly after picking. Tubers keep for a few days in a cool, dark place, but begin to dry out quite quickly.

How to eat
Tubers can be eaten raw or cooked, while the leaves make a delicious herb, and the seeds an aromatic spice.

- The leaves can be used instead of parsley in any dish.
- The seeds are similar to cumin in flavour and are great for Indian-style curries, falafel, or Mexican black bean dishes.
- Thinly slice the crisp raw tubers and add to salads.
- Tubers become sweeter and more chestnut-like when cooked: enjoy them roasted in their skins or steamed and mashed with lots of cream and butter.

How to preserve
When seed heads turn brown and papery, cut them and hang somewhere cool and dry for 2 weeks, then tap out the seeds. They will keep well in an airtight container for many months.

Roots are ready for harvesting once the first frosts of autumn have killed the leaves.

Skirret

Level 2 moderate

Sium sisarum

This long-forgotten root vegetable was once highly prized in the 16th century and well deserves a comeback. The taste is somewhere between a parsnip and a carrot, with a lingering peppery finish, and is best appreciated raw in salads or after gentle pan-frying.

What is it?

Skirret is grown for its long, slender, swollen roots, which form a cluster at the base of the stem just below ground level. A native of Northern Europe and East Asia, skirret was first cultivated by the Romans, then regained popularity in medieval times, and was a mainstay of 16th-century cuisine in both sweet and savoury dishes. With its dark, glossy leaves and tall spikes of lacy white flowers, which are highly attractive to bees and butterflies, skirret makes a wonderful addition to both the flower border and veg patch.

The Roman emperor Tiberius was so fond of skirret, he demanded it as a tribute from vanquished German tribes of the Rhine.

Other root crops can suffer a drop in yield if they run to flower, but skirret roots will keep on growing.

How do I grow it?

Skirret is a very hardy perennial plant and a single planting of just a few specimens will give you harvests for many years. You can either buy a crown of roots from specialist nurseries or raise them from seed, which can be sown under cover or directly outdoors once the soil has warmed. Germination can be erratic, so be sure to sow plenty of seed. Skirret will thrive in most places but prefers damp, rich soil. It is found by streams in the wild and needs plenty of water, or the roots become woody. Provided you keep plants weed free, they can be left to flower without any reduction in cropping.

Quick guide

Plant crowns or sow seeds under cover from early spring

Minimum -10°C (14°F) to maximum 25°C (77°F)

Grow in a sunny or partially shady spot in moist, rich soil

Keep well watered: soil around the roots should never dry out

Plants grow up to 1.25m (4ft) in height and can spread to 60cm (24in)

Harvest roots in autumn as needed or store in damp sand

Step-by-step growing »

Step-by-step growing

Skirret can be grown by planting crowns or dormant roots in early spring, or by raising plants from seed. Grow in good, well-drained soil in a sunny position. Frequent watering will lead to tender, tasty roots.

When to grow and harvest
Plant or sow from early spring for harvesting the following autumn and winter.

	early winter	late winter	early spring	late spring	early summer	late summer	early autumn	late autumn
sow indoors			•	•				
sow outdoors				•	•			
plant out			•	•	•			
harvest	•	•					•	•

1 Prepare the soil

Choose a site in a sunny or partially shady area. Skirret prefers a rich, light, well-drained soil, so dig over the planting site and fork in plenty of well-rotted organic matter to enrich the soil and improve its structure. Allow 2 to 3 weeks before planting for the soil to settle. Rake the soil level, removing any weeds and large stones before planting.

A rich, well-fertilised soil will produce the best-quality crop for harvesting.

2 Plant crowns or sow seeds

Plant crowns in spring as soon as possible after you get them. If the ground is frozen or waterlogged, they can be temporarily stored wrapped in damp cloth or hessian in a cool place. Plant crowns in rows 30cm (12in) apart, leaving the same distance between the crowns. Plant them so that the pinkish growing tips are level with the surface of the soil. Firm in the crowns but avoid compacting the soil, then water in well.

Alternatively, sow seeds under cover in pots of soil-based compost from early to mid- or late spring. Germination takes between 6 and 20 days at 10–22°C (50–72°F). Grow on in a moderately cool place. Transplant the seedlings or sow seeds directly outdoors once the soil has warmed up enough, though germination can be erratic. Sow seeds 2cm (¾in) apart in drills 30cm (12in) apart, and thin out to a final spacing of 30cm (12in).

Crowns should be planted at soil level to prevent crown rot.

③ Aftercare

Keep plants well watered to prevent the roots becoming tough and inedible. Water before the onset of a spell of dry weather so that growth is not checked. Feed with a liquid general fertilizer only if plants are lacking in vigour. Aphids can be a problem and should be removed by hand or tackled with an organic insecticide. Skirret self-seeds freely, but you can also collect the seeds by snapping off mature seed heads and storing them in a paper bag in a cool, dry place, until they dry out and shed their seeds.

Aphids can be rubbed off by hand if the infestation is light.

Cook's tips

Keep fresh

When ready to eat, wrap the lifted roots in paper and store in the fridge.

How to eat

Too delicate to peel, the roots need to be well scrubbed, especially if eating raw.

- Grate or finely slice and eat raw in a salad; goes well with spicy leaves such as rocket or watercress.
- Cube the roots and fry in butter with a little garlic.
- Combine parboiled skirret with grated apple, flour, and eggs to make fritters.
- Use instead of parsnips in a curried soup, or spiced with nutmeg and cinnamon.
- Finely slice and bake with cream for a seasonal gratin.

How to preserve

Skirret roots will keep for several months before transferring to the fridge for cooking and eating. Lift and store layered in boxes of damp sand in a cool shed or cellar. Alternatively, leave in the ground over winter and lift as needed, marking the spot with a cane so they can easily be found.

④ Harvest

Harvest from autumn, once the tops have died back, by lifting the plants. Remove the best roots for eating and then select a few of the straightest, largest roots, without a woody core, for planting in spring the following year. Store roots in a layer of barely moist sand, so they don't dry out. Alternatively, they are happy being left in the ground over winter until needed, though check they are not being eaten by hungry rodents.

{ } **Level 1** easy

Elephant garlic

Allium ampeloprasum var. ampeloprasum

Given the right care and conditions, elephant garlic can produce truly gargantuan bulbs. Yet the cloves have a surprisingly subtle flavour that won't elephant-charge your taste buds: milder and sweeter than traditional garlic, they are ideal for roasting and baking.

What is it?

Despite its name, elephant garlic is actually more closely related to leeks. The broad, flat leaves are a giveaway, as are the large, globe-shaped flowers borne on the end of tall, straight stems. In fact, the bright purple flowers are so pretty, you are most likely to find elephant garlic growing in the flower border alongside other ornamental alliums. Sadly, flowering is detrimental to bulb growth, and flower spikes should be broken off to direct the plants' energies into forming plate-busting bulbs. They need not be wasted, however, as the flower buds and stems (or "scapes") make a tasty early harvest in their own right.

Brought to the US by Balkan immigrants in the 1860s, elephant garlic was thought lost to cultivation until found growing wild in Oregon in the 1940s.

Cloves can be planted directly outdoors or started off under cover in individual pots, before being planted out.

How do I grow it?

To grow elephant garlic, split off individual cloves from a bulb and plant them in rows. How early you plant the cloves is key to the kind of harvest you can expect. Planted early enough in the autumn, the cloves will swell and then divide to produce large bulbs formed of multiple cloves. Planted in midwinter or later, they will form single bulbs and won't develop cloves. However, if you leave these later crops in the ground they will continue to grow and divide the following year. Plants need to be kept well watered, but dislike waterlogging in winter. Try growing them on ridges or in raised beds if this is a problem. They also do not take kindly to competition, so you will need to keep the soil as weed-free as possible. Elephant garlic does not flourish on acidic soils. If you're not certain of your soil type, test it with a pH kit and fork in lime if necessary.

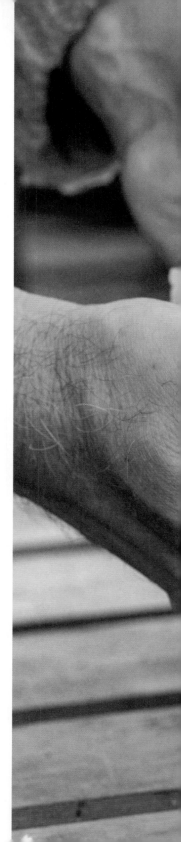

Bulbs can grow to 20cm (8in) in diameter, weigh over 1kg (2¼lb), and produce cloves measuring 5 x 10cm (2 x 4in).

Quick guide

Plant cloves in early to mid-autumn, or late winter at the latest

Minimum 1°C (34°F) to maximum 30°C (86°F)

Grow in a sheltered, open, sunny site on free-draining soil

Keep moist, watering before the onset of dry weather, and stop 3 weeks before harvesting

Rake general fertilizer into the soil before planting

Lift bulbs when the leaves start to yellow

Step-by-step growing »

Step-by-step growing

Each enormous clove can grow to at least the size of a normal bulb. To achieve such results, grow in light, free-draining soil in warm sunshine, provide plenty of moisture but prevent waterlogging, and keep weed free.

When to grow and harvest
Plant in autumn or spring, and harvest once the stems shrivel from mid- to late summer onwards.

	early winter	late winter	early spring	late spring	early summer	late summer	early autumn	late autumn
grow indoors	●	●	●					
plant			●	●			●	●
harvest					●	●		

1 Grow from cloves

If you are planting in their final positions outdoors in autumn, split the bulb up into individual cloves and plant them with the narrow end uppermost, 4cm (1½in) deep and at the spacing described in step 2.
If you have missed the autumn window, live in an area with cold winters, or if the planting site has a tendency to become waterlogged, it can be useful to start plants off under cover instead. Plant the cloves in medium pots in general compost.

Place pots under cover in a cool, bright location and keep the compost moist.

2 Plant out

Once plants started under cover have developed a good length of stem, and the soil has warmed up a little, plant them out 15cm (6in) apart and with 30cm (12in) between rows. Protect from birds with netting or horticultural fleece until established. They dislike competition so keep the soil weed free. Weed by hand or use an onion hoe designed for weeding in tight spaces, so as not to damage the developing bulbs.

Gently tease out the roots of plants started in pots before firming in their planting holes.

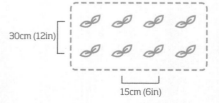

Grow plants at 15cm (6in) intervals with double the distance between rows.

③ Aftercare

Keep crops well watered, particularly before the onset of drought. Continue weeding regularly, removing the weeds at seedling or juvenile stage before they start to compete with the elephant garlic and rob the developing bulbs of moisture and nutrients.

Watch growing plants for signs of flowering stems and cut any stems back by half to prevent them running to seed, which will diminish the size of the bulbs.

④ Harvest

Harvest bulbs after the leaves have turned yellow and died back. Lift bulbs carefully, ease them from the ground with a trowel to avoid any damage, then rub off the soil or wash carefully and allow them to dry. They will store for at least 3 months provided they are not damaged or diseased, so inspect closely and discard or use immediately any suspect bulbs. Check stored bulbs regularly and use any that show signs of deterioration.

Leave any small but healthy plants in the ground and they will continue to grow the following year like a perennial, and the bulbs will divide into cloves and bulk up for harvest.

Cook's tips

Keep fresh
Store elephant garlic bulbs in a cool, dark, dry place with good air circulation. Do not refrigerate.

How to eat
It is a great addition to a dish when a sweeter, subtle garlic flavour is needed.

- Roughly peel whole bulbs and drizzle olive oil inside, then wrap in foil and roast with seasonal vegetables.
- Gently fry chopped cloves as the base for a risotto or pasta sauce for a distinctive flavour.
- Make aïoli sauce with puréed raw cloves - great with steak, grilled chicken, or roasted root vegetables.
- Add a smoky depth of flavour to creamy soups by stirring in the pulp of roasted cloves.

How to preserve
Wrap whole, chopped, or crushed cloves in kitchen film or foil and place in a polythene bag in the freezer, breaking pieces off as needed. Freezing changes the flavour, however, and is not to everyone's liking.

Daylilies

Hemerocallis spp.

Level 1 easy

Daylilies are easy to grow and their gorgeous, exotic-looking flowers will brighten any garden. There are thousands of cultivars to choose from, all of them edible. The buds and open flowers are most commonly used in cooking, but the leaf stems, young shoots, and roots are edible, too.

What is it?

Daylilies are perennial plants that grow for many years from special underground roots called rhizomes. Cultivated in China for centuries as medicinal and food plants, they are grown mainly as an ornamental plant in the West. Their trumpet-like flowers come in an impressive range of colours, from pale apricot to deep purple, and though each flower lasts for only a day, they are produced in abundance over a very long flowering season. The open flowers are the most nutritious, but they can be eaten at any time from bud to just-wilted bloom.

> *Daylilies are mentioned in one of the earliest collections of Chinese folk songs, which dates back to the philosopher Confucius (551–479 BCE).*

The unopened buds, flowers, and wilted blooms can all be eaten and have a fresh flavour that is similar to green beans with a generous dash of spice.

How do I grow it?

Daylilies look wonderful planted in groups in the flower border. Smaller, less vigorous varieties do well in pots, which can be positioned close to home to enjoy those that have a heady fragrance. Choose plants carefully, as late-flowering varieties are less likely to be attacked by the hemerocallis gall midge. The common orange daylily, *Hemerocallis fulva*, is the best all-rounder for eating, with delicious young shoots and roots, as well as stunning, tawny-coloured flowers. Daylilies are generally hardy but vary in their temperature tolerance, so check the label before buying. Plants grown in light shade produce fewer flowers, but the flowers last slightly longer than a day.

Plant container-grown plants any time of year, but preferably in spring

Minimum -40°C (-40°F) to maximum 30°C (86°F)

Grow in sun or light shade in fertile, moist, free-draining, neutral to slightly acidic soil

Water well, if needed, from spring until buds appear

Size varies between cultivars; some can reach 1m (3ft) in height and spread

Pick flowers as needed; harvest new shoots in spring and rhizomes in autumn

Step-by-step growing »

Most flowers open from early morning, but nocturnal varieties open in the evening and last through the night.

Step-by-step growing

Daylily blooms may not be long-lasting, but they are frequent and delicious. Plants can be raised from seed, grown from rhizomes, or young plants can be bought from a nursery or garden centre.

When to grow and harvest

Container plants and those raised from rhizomes are best planted in spring or autumn.

	early winter	late winter	early spring	late spring	early summer	late summer	early autumn	late autumn
sow indoors			•	•				
plant out			•	•	•	•	•	•
harvest			•		•	•	•	

① Sow indoors

Seeds need a period of cold before sowing to break dormancy. Put the seeds in damp sand in a freezer bag and pop in the fridge at 4°C (39°F) for six weeks. Then in spring, sow seeds 13mm (½in) deep into moist, well-drained seed compost kept at 13–20°C (55–68°F). Germination takes 21–49 days. When large enough to handle, transplant seedlings to 8cm (3in) pots and grow on. Harden off the young plants (see p.62) and plant them outdoors after danger of frost has passed, or wait until the weather and soil warm up.

Leave in pots and do not plant out until the danger of frost has passed.

② Plant out

Before planting, prepare the ground by improving the soil with well-rotted organic matter, adding sharp sand and gypsum to clay soils for better structure and drainage, if necessary. Dig a planting hole slightly larger than the pot in which the daylily is planted, and scatter a root-booster of mycorrhizal fungi into the bottom of the planting hole. Remove the daylily from its pot, tease out the roots to encourage them to grow outwards, and plant at the same depth that it was in the container.

Clear all weeds before planting to reduce competition for water and nutrients.

Raising from rhizomes

Daylilies can also be grown from the bare rhizomes, which can be bought in packets from nurseries and garden centres. Only buy roots that are plump and show a few buds or small shoots. Plant them into pots of multi-purpose compost, water well, and put them in a cold frame, cold greenhouse, or by a sheltered wall to bulk up. Always keep the compost moist. Transplant the plants into their final positions the following spring or autumn.

③ Aftercare and harvest

Mulch in spring with well-rotted organic matter such as homemade compost, manure, or leaf mould. If your plants lack vigour, feed with controlled-release fertilizer in spring to boost growth before mulching. Harvest buds and flowers as they appear in summer. Leaves taste better when they are emerging in early spring.

All but the most faded flowers are suitable for eating, and the more you pick the more they bloom.

④ Dividing

Rejuvenate large, established clumps of daylilies by dividing them in autumn or spring. Carefully dig the clump out of the ground and use two forks to ease the roots apart. Remove sections from the edge of the clump, 10–15cm (4–6in) in size, and replant these sections, leaving 30cm (12in) between each one.

Dividing daylilies provides a good opportunity to harvest some of the edible rhizomes.

Cook's tips

Keep fresh

Seal buds and flowers in a polythene bag and keep them in the salad drawer of the fridge.

How to eat

Buds and flowers are used extensively in Asian cuisine, but the rhizomes and young shoots are edible too.

- Strip the petals and use to add colour to a salad.
- Sauté the buds in a little oil or butter and serve as a side dish.
- For a starter or tapas dish, dip buds and partly opened flowers in a light batter and deep fry. Serve with a dipping sauce or sprinkled with salt.
- Use in a Chinese-style bone broth spiced with ginger.
- Young shoots have a mild taste of onion and can be cooked as a side dish or added to stir-fries.
- Smaller rhizomes taste a little like sweet potatoes and can be eaten raw, sautéed, or roasted.

How to preserve

Buds and flowers can be dried in a dehydrator or very low oven, and then rehydrated in hot water for 30 minutes before cooking.

GRAINS
AND SEEDS

Amaranthus caudatus is known for its bright, tassel-like flowers and pale green leaves. It thrives in a sunny spot.

{ Level 1 easy }

Amaranth
Amaranthus caudatus

A combination of brightly coloured leaves, stems, and flowers makes amaranth a very pretty crop to grow. Robust, vigorous, and productive, the plant has edible seeds packed with goodness and amino acids, making amaranth a superfood that is well worth growing.

What is it?

Amaranth is a tall, upright plant that is easy to grow. From the top of the main stem erupts a prominent, pink, cascading flower head, composed of numerous tassels, from which the edible seeds develop. Once a staple grain crop of the Incas, it was forgotten for centuries after the Spanish conquest, but has now been rediscovered in the West as a gluten-free grain rich in health-giving vitamins and minerals, ideal for making flat breads or using as popping "corn".

> Amaranth is a protein powerhouse: just a handful of seeds contains as much protein as a glass of cow's milk.

The young leaves can also be eaten much like spinach, though they have a sharper, slightly sweeter taste.

How do I grow it?

As a spectacular, highly ornamental plant, amaranth is at home in both the flower border and vegetable patch. Give it plenty of space, as it grows densely and shades surrounding plants, and in cooler climates amaranth will need shelter and plenty of sunshine. Seeds germinate easily and can be sown directly into the ground once the soil is warm, or started off under cover. Amaranth can adapt to a wide range of soils, but growth is more compact and it is more likely to flower and crop well in impoverished soils, even in poor summers. Grown to maximize cropping, its water requirements are low. If you are cultivating specimens primarily for their looks, however, give them rich soil and plenty of water; they will tend to flower later.

Step-by-step growing »

Step-by-step growing

Amaranth plants are easily raised from seed. If you have any spare seed left over, use it to grow nutty-tasting microgreens in a tray of compost placed on a sunny windowsill.

When to grow and harvest

Sow in spring, harvest leaves as needed, and allow some plants to mature for harvesting seeds.

	early winter	late winter	early spring	late spring	early summer	late summer	early autumn	late autumn
sow indoors			•	•	•	•	•	
sow outdoors				•	•			
plant				•	•			
harvest				•	•	•	•	•

1 Sow seed

For early planting, sow indoors in modules to avoid seed disturbance, in a propagator, on a warm windowsill, or in a greenhouse at around 20°C (68°F). Transfer the seedlings carefully into larger pots as needed. Alternatively, once the soil is warm, sow the seed directly into finely raked soil. Either scatter the seed evenly in areas where it is to grow in groups, or sow it in rows in shallow drills, 20–30cm (8–12in) apart, then lightly cover it with soil, compost, or vermiculite.

Amaranth grows rapidly, going from seedling to mature plant in 10–12 weeks.

2 Transplant

Acclimatize indoor-sown plants to the colder temperatures outside by placing them in a cloche or cold frame and gradually increasing ventilation first during the day and then also at night. Once all danger of frost has passed, transplant the young plants into their final positions. Choose a sunny, sheltered location in free-draining soil; add a little grit to improve drainage, if needed, and clear the site of weeds. In cooler climates, crops can be grown in a border within a greenhouse or in a polytunnel. Space plants at intervals of 30–40cm (12–16in) in rows 20–30cm (8–12in) apart. Good spacing is important for helping to minimize the risk of downy mildew.

Use your hand to firm the soil around the stem, then water the plants in well.

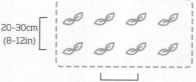

20–30cm (8–12in)

30–40cm (12–16in)

Leave plenty of space between plants so that they do not shade their neighbours.

③ Aftercare

Keep the plants weed-free and water in periods of drought. Apply a mulch around the base of the plants to retain moisture and warmth. Pinch out the growing tips when 20cm (8in) tall to promote bushiness. Feed with dilute liquid tomato fertilizer every 2 to 3 weeks to encourage flowering.

Support plants, if necessary, by tying them into sturdy stakes or canes.

④ Harvest

After approximately 3 months of growth the plants should be mature and the seeds ready to harvest. Seeds fall freely when they are ripe, and just a light nudge of the flowering tassles will dislodge them. Harvest them on a dry day, by bending the flower stem slowly over a clean bucket, and then vigorously shaking or rubbing the seed heads together. Finally, remove the chaff by riddling through a fine sieve, and leave the seeds on a tray to dry.

Remove the chaff to reveal the seeds, which are here red but they also come in white, beige, or black.

The deep red flowers that bloom in the summer make amaranth ideal ornamental as well as edible plants.

Cook's tips

Keep fresh

Eat leaves fresh, or store in a sealed polythene bag, or wrapped in kitchen towel in the salad drawer of the fridge for a few days.

How to eat

Seeds can be eaten as a breakfast cereal, popped in hot oil, mixed with grains, or added to soups, stews, and stir-fries. Leaves can be steamed or eaten raw in salads; young stems can be cooked.

- To use amaranth as a cooked "grain", cover with water, bring to the boil, and simmer for approximately 20 minutes.
- Use the cooked grain instead of tabbouleh in a herby salad.
- The cooked seeds make a creamy porridge: just heat in milk and add nuts and fruit.
- Give dairy desserts a light crunch with popped amaranth.
- Fry leaves and steamed stems with garlic, cumin, and chilli for a light side dish.

How to preserve

Dried seed lasts for months in an airtight container stored in a cool, dark, dry place.

{ Level 1 easy }

Quinoa

Chenopodium quinoa

Quinoa (pronounced "keen-wa") is a cereal crop with a range of coloured seed heads, which vary according to the variety from green to deep red. It is easy to grow, tolerant of the cold, and highly nutritious. Seeds can be boiled as an alternative to rice or ground into a gluten-free flour, and the leaves are edible too.

What is it?

Quinoa is a fast growing annual in the same family of plants as amaranth, spinach, and fat hen. Also known as Inca wheat, it was first cultivated as a crop by the Incas of Peru, and to signify the start of the growing season the Inca Emperor would plant the first sacred seeds with a golden spade. Nearly 500 years later it is esteemed once again by dietitians and foodies as a superfood with a full complement of amino acids, which makes it an excellent vegan source of complete protein.

When to grow and harvest

Start sowing in early spring and harvest from late summer when the seeds have matured.

	early winter	late winter	early spring	late spring	early summer	late summer	early autumn	late autumn
sow indoors			●	●	●			
sow outdoors				●	●			
plant out				●	●			
harvest							●	●

How do I grow it?

Quinoa is straightforward to grow and germinates easily. Sow early if growing for seeds as later sowings will provide only a harvest of leaves. If your growing season is short, feed plants with tomato fertilizer to stimulate flower production.

1 Prepare the soil

Rich, free-draining soils produce the highest yields, so improve the soil a few weeks in advance of sowing or planting out by digging in plenty of well-rotted organic matter. Don't overdo it, however, or plants may produce leafy growth at the expense of seeds. Allow the ground to settle and make sure the soil is clear of all weeds; if sowing directly outdoors, rake the soil into a fine seedbed.

Pick tender young leaves for eating raw in salads; the tougher, older leaves can be cooked and eaten like spinach.

Cook's tips

Keep fresh

Store dry seed in an airtight container in a cool, dark place.

How to eat

Seeds must be boiled for 10–15 minutes before they are ready to eat. Enoy it as a substitute for rice or as a gluten-free alternative to pasta, couscous, and bulgur.

- Give soups a nutrient boost by adding dry quinoa before pouring in the stock.
- Mix with mashed beans, eggs, and herbs and spices to make a veggie burger.
- Stir through roast vegetables and top with a tahini sauce.

How to preserve

Dry seeds can last 3 years in an airtight container.

② Grow from seed

Sow under cover in small pots placed in a propagator set at 18–24°C (64–75°F), sowing 5mm (¼in) deep in seed compost. Harden off seedlings (see p.62), then transplant outdoors after the last frosts, leaving 35cm (14in) between plants and at least 60cm (24in) between rows. You can also sow directly outdoors once the soil has warmed. High temperatures can induce dormancy, however, and if this is the case, shade the soil, sow in the evening, or water before sowing.

③ Aftercare and harvest

Keep plants well watered and free of weeds, and provide support if needed. Harvest on a sunny day after the seeds turn yellow and start to fall. Cut off the seed heads carefully, leaving a bit of stem as a handle, and dry them on trays or in a paper bag in a warm, dry place. After 2 weeks, rub the seed heads so the seeds fall, and pass through a fine sieve. Just before using, rinse the seeds in water to wash off the bitter taste they produce to deter predators.

Chia
Salvia hispanica

Level 1 *easy*

Chia, once a lost crop of the Aztecs, is now a plant with a top billing. The seeds contain more omega-3 fatty acids than salmon, a wealth of antioxidants, minerals, a complete source of protein, and more fibre than flaxseed. Dubbed "the ultimate superfood" by advocates, athletes, and ultra-runners, now it's your turn to feel the power!

What is it?

Chia seeds are harvested from the plant *Salvia hispanica,* a tall, upright, annual with bright green leaves and spikes of blue flowers that appear in summer. It is native to southern Mexico and Guatemala, and the Aztecs and Mayans are believed to have relied heavily on chia seeds as sustenance during hunting and harvesting periods. Plants need a hot, sunny position and a long summer to give enough time for the seeds to mature.

> *Chia is a species in the Salvia genus, which also includes the herb sage and as many as 900 ornamental flowering plants.*

Harvest the seeds by gathering the flowering spikes once the flowers are over and the seed heads have dried.

How do I grow it?

Chia plants are best raised from seed sown early indoors, unless your climate is warm enough to sow directly outdoors from early spring. Plants need moisture-retentive, moderately fertile, free-draining, light soil, and a position in full sun where the soil will warm up quickly in spring. The light blue flowers would make a valuable addition to an ornamental flower border. Plants also grow well in containers of gritty compost, making it ideal for a patio or balcony. If possible, grow plants in a sheltered position near a wall to take advantage of radiated heat.

Chia bears attractive blue flowers in upright spikes, but only once there are fewer than 12 hours of daylight.

Quick guide

Sow seeds indoors in spring and transplant when there is no danger of frost

Minimum 11°C (52°F) to maximum 36°C (97°F)

Grow in a sheltered, sunny position, on free-draining soil

Keep moist to slightly dry; do not over water

Plants reach 1.2m (4ft) high and 40cm (16in) across

Gather the mature seed heads from summer till autumn

Step-by-step growing ≫

Step-by-step growing

Start chia plants off under cover and plant out in a sunny spot in light, fertile soil. Keep the soil moist, but never waterlogged, and pinch out shoots to encourage branching.

 ## 1 Sow indoors

Sow indoors in spring, about a month before the frosts end in your area. Sow the tiny seeds into moist seed compost and lightly cover by sieving over a fine layer of compost or vermiculite. Place in a warm greenhouse or propagator set to 21–25°C (70–77°F) until germinated. Keep the compost moist and transplant the strongest seedlings into individual pots of loam-based or multi-purpose compost. Continue growing under cover, potting on to larger pots as needed. Seedlings are ready for planting out when they are 8–10cm (3–4in) tall.

Chia seeds germinate in about 7 days and can be transplanted, with the aid of a dibber, when large enough to handle.

2 Plant out

Once all risk of frost has passed, harden off the young plants for a week or so by placing them outdoors during the day and returning them to shelter at night. Alternatively, transfer the plants to a cold frame and prop the lid open during the day, shutting it again at night. Once acclimatized, plant out at 60cm (24in) intervals in rows 90cm (36in) apart.

You can also directly sow seeds outside after the last frosts and when the soil has warmed enough. Sow into a raked-over seedbed, either in drills or broadcast, and sow more than you need. Lightly cover, keep moist, and progressively thin out until you are left with the strongest plants 60cm (24in) apart.

Transfer acclimatized plants to a sunny location outdoors.

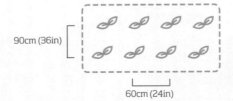

90cm (36in)

60cm (24in)

Chia plants grow tall and bushy, and need plenty of space around them.

3 Aftercare

Chia doesn't like competition for water and nutrients, so keep on top of the weeding until plants are established, and water regularly. It is worth applying a thick mulch of well-rotted organic matter to suppress weeds and help lock in moisture.

Chia plants have a tendency to grow tall and leggy, but you can prevent this by pinching out the tips to encourage branching and bushier growth. When a plant has produced 4 leaves, pinch out the growing tip just above a leaf. This causes sideshoots to form, which should then also be pinched out once they have produced 3–4 leaves.

Plants can grow as tall as 2m (6ft) and on windy sites may need tying in to stakes or canes for support.

4 Harvest

Harvest seeds by gathering flower spikes when most of the petals have fallen. Place in open paper bags and leave in a warm, airy place to dry out. Crush the dried seed heads to release the seeds and sieve out the chaff. Chia is a short-day plant and needs fewer than 12 hours of daylight to initiate flower and seed production. In cooler northerly climates short days come too late in the season, and plants are frosted before seeds can be set. You can, however, gather the leaves throughout the growing season to make infusions.

Cook's tips

Keep fresh

Store seeds in an airtight container in a cool, dark, dry place. Fresh leaves are best used immediately.

How to eat

Dry seeds can be added to bakes or scattered over any number of dishes for a crunchy nutrient boost. Soaked in liquid, the seeds swell and take on a gloopy texture that works well in desserts and porridge.

- Use in place of poppy seeds in recipes for cakes, loaves, flat breads, and crackers.
- Stir a tablespoon into a few handfuls of oats and leave to soak in milk overnight for an extra-creamy bowl of cereal in the morning.
- Add soaked seeds to milky or creamy desserts, such as rice pudding and fruit fools.
- Pour boiling water over chopped fresh or dried leaves for an invigorating tea.

How to preserve

Seeds can last for 5 years stored as described above. Chopped leaves can be dried in a dehydrator or very low oven and used for tea.

Quick guide

Sow indoors, harden off carefully, and plant out only once the last frost has passed

Minimum 23°C (73°F) to maximum 30°C (86°F)

Sesame will flourish in warm, moist, free-draining soil

Water when soil or compost is dry, but do not over water

Plants grow up to 90cm (35in) tall and spread to 50cm (20in)

Harvest when pods turn brown, just before the seeds are shed

{ Level 2 moderate }

Sesame
Sesamum indicum

You may be surprised to discover that the seeds found on top of a burger bun come from a highly ornamental plant bearing flowers very similar in apperance to a foxglove. Once pollinated, the flowers develop into green, torpedo-shaped pods containing the nutritious seeds that are so high in cholesterol-lowering "good" fats.

What is it?

A tall, upright, annual plant native to tropical India, sesame bears elongated oval leaves and attractive pink or white flowers that grow in threes at the junction of the main and leaf stems. Seeds range in colour from cream to black or red, and can be eaten whole or crushed for their oil. The seeds have been munched for centuries; records exist on ancient Assyrian tablets and in the writings of Marco Polo of sesame being grown as a crop, long before burgers and Sesame Street were invented.

When to grow and harvest

Sow indoors in spring and plant out when soil and weather are warm. Harvest from late summer, depending on climate.

	early winter	late winter	early spring	late spring	early summer	late summer	early autumn	late autumn
sow indoors			●	●				
sow outdoors				●	●			
plant out					●			
harvest						●	●	

As well as being full of healthy fats, sesame seeds are also high in fibre, metabolism-boosting vitamin B1, and an assortment of minerals.

How do I grow it?

Sesame is a warm-climate crop but can be grown outdoors in temperate areas with long, hot summers, or raised in the greenhouse. Grow in a sheltered, sunny spot, ideally close to a sunny wall to benefit from the radiated heat.

① Sow indoors

Sow indoors 6 weeks before the last frost, 1cm (½in) deep in modules or trays of moist, well-drained seed compost, covered to block out the light. Keep in a propagator heated to 22–25°C (72–77°F) and mist the compost with tepid water to maintain dampness. Germination takes 7–14 days. Remove the cover as soon as the seedlings emerge and place in a sunny spot or windowsill. Water lightly with tepid water when the compost is dry.

Cook's tips

Keep fresh
Dry seeds thoroughly and store in an airtight jar in a cool, dark place.

How to eat
Use whole seeds raw or toasted, or grind to a paste. Thinnings can also be used as a microgreen.

- Make tahini by grinding the seeds with a little oil.
- Toast seeds in a dry frying pan and sprinkle over salads, fish dishes, or roasted vegetables.
- Stir into a flapjack mix or use as a topping for bread.

How to preserve
Double-bag seeds before freezing to avoid flavour taint from other foods.

❷ Plant and sow outdoors

Harden off carefully (see p.62) and plant out at least 2 weeks after the last frost, spacing plants 15-20cm (6-8in) apart. You can also sow directly outdoors at this point. Sow in drills and sow more than you need, thinning plants to 15-20cm (6-8in) apart. Plants can also be grown on in containers filled with a mix of mulit-purpose and John Innes No.3 compost.

❸ Aftercare and harvest

Sesame is very drought tolerant; keep the soil moist, erring on the dry side, but never waterlogged. Plants grown in cooler climates will benefit from a feed of high-potash fertilizer. The seed pods form inside the fading flowers. Harvest as the pods start to dry out and before they split. Leave on a tray in a warm, airy place to dry, then gently crack open the pods and remove the seeds.

Quick guide

Sow indoors, or outdoors when the soil is warm enough

Minimum 5°C (41°F) to maximum 30°C (86°F)

Grow in a fertile, moist, free-draining soil on a warm, sheltered, sunny site

Keep crops well watered

Plants grow up to 1.25m (4ft) tall

Pick cobs when the tassels have darkened

{ Level 2 moderate }

Strawberry popcorn

Zea mays Everta Group

This popping variety of maize bears ruby-red kernels on miniature cobs that can be popped whole and the popcorn eaten straight from the husk – popcorn-on-the-cob, anyone? If that doesn't appeal, the dried cobs make pretty decorations.

What is it?

Maize or corn is an annual plant belonging to the same family of grasses as wheat and lawn grass. Popping corn is the same species as sweetcorn, but comes from the Everta Group selected for the hard outer hulls to their kernels, which rupture explosively when the starch inside is heated to a sufficient degree. Evidence for the sale of popping corn dates back to the 1820s, and by 1848 the word "popcorn" had appeared in the dictionary.

Although humans have been popping corn for over 3,000 years, the first commercial popcorn machine was invented in Chicago in 1885.

Known as "silks", the female flowers grow from the ears of the plant and catch pollen produced by the "male" flowers at the top.

How do I grow it?

This variety only grows to 1.25m (4ft) tall and is ideal for growing in a small garden or containers. To do well, strawberry popcorn needs a long, warm growing season and moisture-retentive, free-draining soil. Dig in plenty of well-rotted organic matter where you are going to plant, or use ground that has been improved for a previous crop. It is also helpful to warm the soil where you are going to grow your crops by laying black polythene over it for a few weeks before planting out. If you have space, or are simply a big fan of popcorn, make repeat sowings every 2 weeks until midsummer, to extend the harvesting season. Watering is particularly beneficial at the point when plants begin to flower, and then again as grains start to swell.

Individual cobs of
strawberry popcorn grow
to around 10–15cm (4–6in)
in length, much smaller
than cobs of regular corn.

Step-by-step
growing »

Step-by-step growing

Sow indoors to extend the season, or outdoors once the soil is warm. Plant in blocks, not rows, and leave pollination to nature, or help by giving plants a gentle shake.

When to grow and harvest

Sow from late winter and harvest from early summer, depending on the weather.

	early winter	late winter	early spring	late spring	early summer	late summer	early autumn	late autumn
sow indoors		●	●					
sow outdoors				●	●			
plant out				●	●			
harvest					●	●	●	

1 Sow indoors

Sow a pair of seeds 2.5–4cm (1–1½in) deep in 7.5cm (3in) pots or modules of moist seed compost. Place on a sunny windowsill, in a greenhouse, or in a propagator set to 20–26°C (68–79°F). Once germinated, thin to leave the strongest seedling. Plants are sensitive to root damage and disturbance, so do this while they are still small and use a trowel or dibber to help you. Once all risk of frost has passed, harden off the young plants to outdoor conditions for a week or so, placing them outside during the day and returning them to shelter at night. Alternatively, transfer to a cold frame and prop the lid open during the day, before shutting it again at night.

The seeds are a favourite food of mice and it is best to protect exposed pots or trays, especially if growing in a greenhouse.

2 Plant out

Once acclimatized, move the young plants to their final growing positions outdoors. Plant 38cm (15in) apart, in rows 45cm (18in) apart.

Strawberry popcorn plants are short for corn, rising to only 1.25m (4ft) tall, which makes them suitable for growing in containers. Fill the pots with John Innes No.3 compost or similar, keep plants well-watered, and feed regularly with liquid general fertilizer until established, then change to a high-potash fertilizer, such as tomato feed.

Seeds can also be sown in situ at around this time. Sow 2 to 3 seeds under cloches or jars at the final spacing, and thin to leave the strongest seedling. You may need to net the sowing area against mice until the seedlings establish.

Plant out the young plants before they start to get pot-bound.

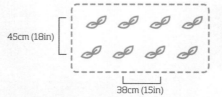

45cm (18in)

38cm (15in)

Plant in rectangular blocks rather than long rows, so the pollen has the best chance of being blown on to neighbouring crops.

3 Aftercare

Protect the young plants with cloches or windbreaks if the weather turns cold. Remove weeds between plants but take care not to damage roots growing near the soil surface. Keep plants well watered when the flowers appear, then again when the cobs are developing, and if there is a spell of drought in the meantime. In windy sites, plants may also need earthing up or staking as they grow tall.

Corn is naturally wind-pollinated, but you can provide a helping hand. When the male flowers at the top of the plant start releasing pollen, you will notice clouds of yellow dust on the lower leaves or when you brush against the plants. Give the stem of each plant a gentle shake to encourage pollen to drop from these male flowers to the silky tassels of the female flowers emerging from the juvenile cobs below. Do this every day until no more pollen is released.

Keep plants well watered until they establish and in periods of drought. Provide additional watering when the flowers appear and cobs begin to form.

4 Harvest

Harvest when the tassels on the cobs have darkened. Since they are popped rather than eaten as corn on the cob, any lack of sweetness isn't the end of the world and it doesn't matter if you pick them a a bit early. At this point, cut the cobs and some stalk and gently remove the outer husk and tassel debris. Hang the picked cobs in a dry, airy place until you're ready to pop.

Plants sown indoors should be ready for picking by early to midsummer.

Cook's tips

Keep fresh

Store in a sealed container, but do not keep in the refrigerator as this can dry out the kernels.

How to eat

Cook them for popping corn. You could leave the cobs to dry out and use them in a decorative display, but this seems a terrible waste! Carefully remove the kernels with a sharp knife, or pop whole cobs at a time.

- Method 1 - Pour enough oil to cover the bottom of a lidded saucepan. Place on a medium heat and add the kernels when the oil is sizzling. Get the lid on quick and keep agitating to avoid burning the kernels. Lift the lid when the popping stops.

- Method 2 - Place cob in a large paper bag and microwave on a high heat for 4-5 minutes.

- Enjoy the popcorn plain, tossed with salt and melted butter, or flavour as desired.

How to preserve

Store cobs and kernels in a sealed container in a cool, dark, dry place, such as a garage, shed, or similar. Do not allow to dry out if using for popcorn.

HERBS AND SPICES

With its attractive fresh green leaves and sweet pea-like flowers, fenugreek will suit an ornamental border.

Fenugreek

Level 1 easy

Trigonella foenum-graecum

Fenugreek is often sown for its nitrogen-fixing abilities as a green manure, but it is well worth growing as a food crop to harvest its pungent, earthy leaves, which are used fresh or dried in many Indian dishes. Allow a few plants to flower and pod for a second harvest of spicy seeds.

What is it?

Fenugreek is an easy-to-grow annual in the same family of plants as peas and beans, with pretty, oval-shaped leaves that grow in sets of three like clover. There are two forms: a large-seeded variety with white flowers, which can only be cut once; and a smaller-seeded variety with slightly smaller leaves and yellow flowers, which will regrow after cutting. Plants produce long, thin, green seed pods like curved beaks, which turn yellow when ripe. Both leaves and seeds are rich in nutrients and fibre, and are reputed to help relieve digestive problems and lower blood-sugar levels.

"Fenugreek" comes from the Latin for "Greek hay", probably because the plant was first cultivated in the Near East and the dried leaves smell a little like hay.

How do I grow it?

Plants have a degree of frost resistance and can be sown outdoors from early spring until well into autumn. Grow in a sunny, sheltered, well-drained position on light, moist, free-draining soil. Fenugreek is a useful crop for growing in small gardens as it doesn't need much space. Plants also do well in containers filled with a mix of John Innes No.3 compost and 30 per cent added multi-purpose compost. If growing the larger variety for its leaves rather than seeds, make repeat sowings as it does not regrow after being cut. The smaller-seeded variety can be grown as a cut-and-come-again crop. Seeds can also be sprouted and grown for microgreens.

Sow seeds outdoors in a fine seedbed. Germination is usually rapid and reliable.

Quick guide

Sow indoors from late winter and outdoors from early spring to early autumn

Minimum 0°C (32°F) to maximum 32°C (90°F)

Choose a sheltered, sunny spot on light, free-draining soil

Not a thirsty crop, but don't let the soil dry out

Grows to 60cm (24in) in height and 40cm (16in) in spread

Harvest leaves once plants are established; leave a few plants to grown on for seeds

Step-by-step growing ›

Step-by-step growing

Grow in light, well-drained soil in a sunny position. Fenugreek does not have a high demand for water, but growth will be more rapid if the soil is kept moderately moist. Protect from pigeons until established.

When to grow and harvest

Make successional sowings throughout the season, especially if you are growing the large-leaved variety for its leaves.

	early winter	late winter	early spring	late spring	early summer	late summer	early autumn	late autumn
sow indoors		•	•					
transplant			•	•				
sow outdoors				•	•	•	•	
harvest						•	•	•	•

1 Sow indoors

If you want an early crop, start plants off indoors in late winter. Fenugreek can get unhappy about being transplanted, so grow the seedlings in modules to minimize root disturbance. Germination is rapid and usually takes less than a week. Carefully pot on the seedlings to individual pots before they start to outgrow their modules. Fenugreek withstands spells at 0°C (32°F), but it is best to wait until after the last frosts before hardening off (see p.62) and planting out indoor-raised seedlings.

Sow one seed to each module so that you do not disturb the roots by thinning out.

2 Plant and sow outdoors

Improve the structure and nutrients at the growing site by digging in well-rotted organic matter, and allow to settle. Transplant seedlings 5cm (2in) apart in rows 20cm (8in) apart. To sow direct, rake the soil to a fine texture and form drills 0.5cm (¼in) deep. Sow seeds thickly and cover lightly. Once seedlings emerge, thin plants to 5cm (2in) apart. Repeat sow seeds of the large-leaved variety once a row has germinated, as it does not regrow after flowering.

Keep the soil around seedlings and young plants free of weeds to help them establish.

20cm (8in)

5cm (2in)

Fenugreek plants don't suffer from being grown close together and the proximity helps to smother weeds.

3 Aftercare and harvest

Cover seedlings and young plants with netting or horticultural fleece to prevent them from being eaten by pigeons. Carefully hoe or remove weeds by hand until plants have established themselves, after which rapid growth acts as a weed-suppressant. Water only if the soil looks dry. Harvest leaves from 6 weeks after sowing, when plants are 25cm (10in) tall or less, and before flowers appear, after which the quality deteriorates. Cut stems just above soil level. The small-leaved variety can be cut several times to keep it productive and prevent seeding.

Leave some plants to flower and produce seed pods for a second harvest of seeds.

4 Harvesting seeds

If growing plants for seeds, you can remove some leaves, but not so many to weaken growth. Harvest the pods once they have turned yellow but before they split. If the pods are wet, dry the seeds on a tray before storing.

Try to harvest after a spell of sunny weather so the seeds will be dry.

Cook's tips

Keep fresh
Store fresh leaves in a polythene bag in the fridge for 2 to 3 days. Plunge in cold water for 30 minutes to refresh wilted leaves.

How to eat
Fresh leaves can be used as a substitute for watercress in salads or lightly cooked and eaten like spinach. Both fresh and dried fenugreek are widely used in Indian cuisine. Look out for recipes with *methi* in the title, which is Hindi for fenugreek.

- Combine with potatoes in the classic Punjabi dish aloo methi.
- Dried leaves are one of the key flavourings for Old Delhi-style butter chicken.
- Stir fresh or dried leaves into dough to flavour flat breads.
- Make a lahmajoun (Armenian pizza) spiced with ground fenugreek and cumin seeds.
- Sprinkle the seeds whole on vegetables to roast.

How to preserve
Dry leaves slowly on trays in a very low oven. Leaves and seeds will keep for a year in airtight containers in a cool, dry place.

{ } Level 1 easy

Wood sorrel

Oxalis acetosella or O. violacea

This diminutive perennial plant, with its fresh, green, clover-like leaves and dainty white spring flowers, is a beautiful addition to gardens with dappled shade. With high levels of oxalic acid, the foliage should not be consumed in large quantities, but as a garnish it is prized for its wonderful sour-apple flavour.

What is it?

Wood sorrel is a common name applied to many species of *Oxalis*, but the delicate natives species of moist woodlands are *Oxalis acetosella* throughout Europe and Central Asia, and *Oxalis violacea* in North America. The trefoil-shaped leaves are thought to be the original shamrock, and are sent up from small rhizomes to form spreading carpets among the leaf litter. They have been a popular plant with foragers for centuries, but, though easy to grow, are not commonly found in gardens. Stock is often available from wildflower nurseries, or plants can be collected from the wild with the landowner's permission.

Another common name for wood sorrel is "Alleluia", so called because the flowers appear between Easter and Pentecost.

The delicate flowers and soft green leaves of wood sorrel open up during the day, then fold up at night to protect themselves from harsh weather.

How do I grow it?

Although wood sorrel is extremely hardy, it is best propagated in the light shade and shelter of a cold frame. This can be done successfully in three ways: by sowing seeds in spring; by planting dormant rhizomes in autumn; or by lifting and dividing existing clumps in spring. Grow in a moist but free-draining site, and enrich the soil with leaf mould before planting out. Once established in a suitable spot, plants will spread quickly, forming a lush mat of leaves to be plucked throughout the growing season.

The leaves of wood sorrel can be plain green or marked with purple, depending on the variety.

Quick guide

Plant rhizomes in autumn and divisions in early spring; sow seed early spring

Minimum -15°C (5°F) to maximum 30°C (86°F)

Grow in full or partial shade in moist, free-draining soil

Water before the onset of drought

Plants grow up to 10cm (4in) high and can spread indefinitely

Harvest flowers in spring and leaves in spring and summer

Step-by-step growing »

Step-by-step growing

Try growing wood sorrel under fruit trees or in quiet, shady corners of the garden where other productive crops are unlikely to thrive. Their low carpet of leaves make ideal ground cover.

When to grow and harvest
Propagate wood sorrel by planting rhizomes in autumn, or by sowing seed, or dividing existing clumps in early spring.

	early winter	late winter	early spring	late spring	early summer	late summer	early autumn	late autumn
sow seeds			•					
plant dormant rhizomes							•	•
plant out				•	•			
harvest				•	•	•	•	
divide plants			•					

1 Raise from rhizomes or seeds

When the rhizomes are dormant in autumn, plant them where they will grow or under cover. Fill a seed tray or modules with a mix of compost and leaf mould, and plant each rhizome 2.5cm (1in) deep. Water well, allow to drain, and place in a cold frame.

Plants can also be raised from seed in seed trays or modules filled with the same mix of compost and leaf mould. Cover lightly with leaf mould, water well, and place in a cold frame. Prick out young plants once large enough to handle and pot up individually to grow on.

The unusual round rhizomes are roughly the size of large peas.

2 Plant out and aftercare

Plants should be ready to put in their final positions by late spring or early summer. Prepare the soil by digging in plenty of leaf mould. Gently tease apart young plants raised in seed trays and plant 10–15cm (4–6in) apart, in clusters rather than rows, to quickly produce a natural-looking carpet as they spread. Water in well and keep the soil moist while they establish, then only during dry spells.

Gently tease out the roots to help plants establish themselves in their new home.

10–15cm (4–6in)

Plant in odd-numbered clusters for a natural look.

③ Harvest

Simply pluck the stems of individual leaves and flowers as required during the growing season, from spring into summer and sometimes autumn in wet climates. Established plants will tolerate having up to one third of their leaves picked without ill effect.

Wood sorrel thrives in shade but can't handle too much competition, so keep the soil free from weeds.

④ Lift and divide clumps

To further propagate wood sorrel, large clumps can be lifted and divided in early spring as they come into growth. Ease them from the ground with a fork and gently pull sections apart. Large pieces do well planted directly in the soil, while smaller divisions are best potted up and brought on in a cold frame.

Cook's tips

Keep fresh
Leaves are best eaten as soon as possible after picking, but will keep wrapped loosely in a polythene bag in the fridge for 2 to 3 days.

How to eat
The fresh, lemon-and-sour-apple flavour really zings in raw leaves, but they also impart a delicate sharp taste when lightly cooked.

- Whip up a simple wood sorrel sauce by cooking leaves briefly in melted butter with cream, lemon juice, and seasoning.
- Scatter over salads to add an acidic note. This works especially well with recipes containing eggs, or rich potato salads.
- Slice finely and combine with whipped cream to make a lovely sharp contrast to indulgent chocolate or custard desserts.
- Add to sautéed wild mushrooms just before serving.

How to preserve
Try freezing the leaves in ice cubes to add to drinks. Or pickle chopped leaves in a mixture of vinegar and sugar (a bit like mint sauce) and keep in the fridge.

Fish mint

Level 1 easy

Houttuynia cordata

The name may not be familiar, but it's likely a form of fish mint already grows in your garden, since the multi-coloured cultivar 'Chameleon' is a popular ground cover plant. It is the plain green species, however, that is such a prized Asian herb, with its red-edged leaves and slightly fishy, coriander-and-orange flavour.

Quick guide

Sow during spring in a cold frame, or plant from spring to autumn

Minimum -15°C (5°F) to maximum 30°C (86°F)

Grow in moist, humus-rich soil in sun or partial shade

Water regularly to keep the soil constantly moist

Plants grow up to 30cm (1ft) tall and spread indefinitely

Harvest young leaves from spring to autumn while plant is in growth

What is it?

This herbaceous perennial hails from Southeast Asia, where it grows in moist, shady places and is widely used as a herb in local cuisine, and as a treatment in traditional Chinese medicine. Western gardeners usually only value fish mint for its attractive carpets of foliage and white summer flowers. It flourishes in moist soils and pond margins, where the plant can easily become invasive thanks to long stems that grow their own roots, which enable it to spread rapidly.

When to grow and harvest

Protect spring-sown seeds in a cold frame for reliable germination, or divide existing plants in spring.

	early winter	late winter	early spring	late spring	early summer	late summer	early autumn	late autumn
sow indoors			•	•				
plant seedlings					•	•		
plant pot-grown			•	•	•	•	•	
harvest				•	•	•	•	

Fish mint spreads at a rapid pace, so if you have limited space just grow in a pot.

How do I grow it?

Fish mint is hardy and easy to grow in soils that do not dry out. It is best grown in containers or planted out in a bucket with the bottom cut out and 8cm (3in) of the rim above ground, otherwise given the right conditions it can becomes invasive.

1 Sow seeds

For reliable germination, seed is best sown in the shelter of a cold frame or cool greenhouse. Fill a seed tray with compost, sow seeds thinly across the surface, and cover lightly with compost, before watering thoroughly and allowing to drain. Keep the compost consistently moist. When seedlings are large enough to handle, gently prick out into 7.5cm (3in) pots and harden them off to acclimatize to outdoor conditions (see p.62).

2 Plant out

Plant seedlings 45cm (18in) apart and water in well. You can also plant container-raised specimens any time from spring to early autumn. Water in generously and during dry weather, until established. Alternatively, grow plants outdoors in large containers to restrict growth; one plant will fill a 30cm (12in) pot. Use peat-free compost with some loam-based compost added to help retain moisture. Water pots regularly; daily in hot summer weather.

3 Aftercare and harvest

In frost-prone areas the roots can be damaged or killed during severe winters, particularly on wet soils and in pots. Protect them by adding a thick mulch of compost once the foliage has died back. Patchy or slow growth is most likely to be due to dry soil conditions and should be remedied by regular watering. Harvest leaves by snipping off the tips of young shoots. Stop picking if leaves become bitter during autumn or are knocked back by frosts.

Quick guide

Sow indoors in spring; plant container-raised plants from spring to early autumn

Minimum -10°C (14°F) to maximum 35°C (95°F)

Grow in damp soil, in sun or partial shade

Keep well watered if not growing in wet ground such as pond margins

Plants grow up to 40cm (16in) high and 90cm (36in) or more across

Harvest whole shoots in late spring and leaves into autumn

Water celery

Level 1 easy

Oenanthe javanica

With a flavour similar to celery, combined with a hint of parsley and carrot, this vigorous perennial is hardy and easy to grow in any pond margin or damp border. While water celery is completely safe to eat, others of the *Oenanthe* genus are extremely toxic, so always check the Latin name on the label before consuming.

What is it?

Water celery is a perennial native to the river banks, lake shores, and paddy fields, of eastern Asia, where it spreads by creeping stems to form large colonies. Its flat umbels of tiny white flowers are typical of the Apiaceae family, which includes cow parsley and carrots. The vitamin- and mineral-rich stems and leaves are eaten across its native range. The young shoots are an esteemed spring vegetable in Japan. It is also a popular ground cover plant for pond margins and readily available in garden centres.

When to grow and harvest

Sow seeds under cover in spring for planting out in summer, or plant container-raised plants throughout the growing season.

	early winter	late winter	early spring	late spring	early summer	late summer	early autumn	late autumn
sow indoors			●	●				
plant seedlings					●	●		
plant pot-grown			●	●	●	●	●	
harvest					●	●	●	●

The pink variegated cultivar 'Flamingo' provides a burst of colour and is just as tasty as the standard green species.

How do I grow it?

Find space for plants at the edge of a pond or in a damp border, where they will quickly form attractive clumps of foliage. Place in full sun for the best displays of the pretty white flowers. Plants tolerate drier soils if given shade and watered well.

 ## 1 Sow seeds

In spring, sow seeds on the surface of moist compost in a seed tray and cover lightly with compost. Place in a cold frame or cool greenhouse and keep damp until seeds germinate; this can take several weeks and is often erratic. When seedlings are large enough to handle, pot them into individual pots and grow on in a cold frame. In summer, harden off the seedlings (see p.62) to acclimatize them to outdoor conditions.

2 Plant out and aftercare

Plant seedlings 75cm (30in) apart and water in well if not in wet soil. Container-raised specimens can be planted any time after the last frosts until autumn. Water well and plant to the same depth as they grew in their pots. These tough plants look after themselves in wet conditions, but need regular watering in drier locations. Remove faded stems and leaves in early winter and apply a thick mulch of compost (unless growing in a pond) to shield roots from frost.

3 Harvest and propagation

In late spring, harvest the entire young stem and leaves by cutting it at the base; stems become tough and unpalatable later in the growing season. Leaves can be picked as a herb into autumn. Water celery spreads by rooting underground stems (stolons), which makes propagation easy as growth begins in late spring. Simply lift and split a section into pieces with healthy roots and shoots. Pot these up and grow on outdoors, ready for planting by late summer.

Beneath the papery skin, the flesh of turmeric rhizomes is deep orange and fragrant.

Turmeric

Curcuma longa

Level 2 moderate

Turmeric spice comes from the rhizomes of the turmeric plant, which are dried and ground into the colourful powder. Fresh turmeric has a more powerful flavour than powder, full of citrus zest and pepperiness, and it is well worth growing plants for a ready supply of rhizomes with superfood health benefits.

What is it?

Turmeric is a perennial plant native to Southeast Asia. From the same family as ginger, turmeric looks similar in growth but the leaves are broader, and it can reach up to 1m (3ft) in height. When added to a curry, dahl, or tagine, turmeric gives an earthy, slightly bitter flavour. Turmeric is known to contain antioxidants, and to have anticarcinogenic effects – its popularity in traditional Ayurvedic medicine has long been established. The reddish-brown colouring from the dried rhizome is also used in the manufacture of cosmetics and dyes for clothing and carpets.

Turmeric leaves can also be used to flavour dishes and have the added benefit of not staining clothes.

How do I grow it?

Turmeric grows best in warm or hot climates, so keep it in a greenhouse if you live somewhere cool. Grow plants in pots of moisture-retentive compost in the greenhouse or as a foliage houseplant. Provide warmth, plenty of water, and a humid atmosphere, and feed during the growing season. Turmeric can be overwintered in a moderately warm greenhouse in a dormant state by drying out the compost. It is usually reluctant to emerge the following year, and may not appear until late spring or even early summer, but do not give up hope!

In Indian weddings, turmeric is applied to the face and arms of the bride and groom as part of the traditional Haldi ceremony.

Quick guide

Plant in pots in spring so they get a full growing season to become established

Minimum 20°C (75°F) to maximum 30°C (86°F)

Grow outdoors in warm climates and in a greenhouse in cooler climates

Keep constantly moist in the growing season; reduce watering in cooler conditions.

Plants can reach 1m (3ft) in height and 60cm (2ft) in spread

Harvest the leaves and rhizomes in spring and summer

Step-by-step growing »

Step-by-step growing

Turmeric is better grown in containers in cooler and temperate climates. Choose a warm and sheltered spot to encourage the best growth, and try to keep a high humidity around the plants.

When to grow and harvest

Plant rhizomes in early spring to break dormancy. Harvest rhizomes at the very end of the growing season.

	early winter	late winter	early spring	late spring	early summer	late summer	early autumn	late autumn
plant rhizomes			●					
transplant				●	●			
harvest							●	●

1 Sprout rhizomes

Begin by breaking the dormancy of the rhizomes. Fill 9cm (3½in) pots with John Innes No.3 compost mixed with 20 per cent multi-purpose compost; this mix holds moisture for longer and conducts heat well. Plant one rhizome to a pot, 5cm (2in) below the surface. Place the pots in a propagator or on heated mats, set to an ideal temperature of 30°C (86°F). Once the rhizomes have sprouted, grow on in a sunny position at 20°C (68°F).

Choose plump and undamaged rhizomes for planting.

2 Grow on and transplant

Keep the compost constantly moist. Transfer plants to their final growing location once growth reaches 20cm (8in). Turmeric needs to be kept at 20°C (68°F) throughout the growing season, so in cooler climates they are best grown on under cover in large containers with several plants to a pot.

Grow on plants in the same moisture-retentive compost mix as you used for sprouting the rhizomes.

③ Aftercare and harvest

Keep the compost moist at all times when in growth. Feed every 2 weeks with a liquid general fertilizer and provide an occasional boost of liquid seaweed.

If growing in containers under cover, regularly mist plants with tepid water to stop the leaf margins from yellowing and to discourage red spider mite, which turn the leaves mottled and yellow, weave fine webs, and thrive in dry air.

Once established, pick leaves only occasionally and not from the same plant. To harvest the rhizomes, wait for the leaves to yellow and start to die back before digging them up.

Container-grown plants can be moved outdoors when temperatures hit 20°C (68°F), but keep misting.

④ Winter care

Plants still in leaf can be overwintered in a warm greenhouse or brought indoors and grown on as a houseplant. Maintain humidity by keeping them in the bathroom, or stand on trays of pebbles filled with water to the bottom of the pot. Mist occasionally. Transplant to pots one size larger in spring once they outgrow their current pots. Rhizomes for sprouting next year can be overwintered in a dormant state in pots of dry compost at 12–15°C (54–59°F), watering occasionally to stop them drying out completely.

{ Level 2 moderate }

Wasabi

Wasabia japonica

The roots of the wasabi plant taste a lot like horseradish and, because it is comparatively slow-growing – hence expensive to produce – most wasabi paste outside of Japan is a fake concoction of horseradish and mustard. Grow your own to avoid imitations!

What is it?

Native to Japan, wasabi is found in boggy ground by misty mountain rivers. A slow-growing, hardy perennial, it has glossy, heart-shaped leaves and spikes of small white flowers in late spring. A well-grown plant can also be a garden feature, and thrives in cool, cloudy summers. The Japanese prize *sawa* (water-grown) wasabi is of higher quality than *oka* (field-grown). Commercial paste is made by grinding dried roots into powder, but finely grated fresh roots provide an even stronger and cleaner taste. Leaves, stalks, flowers, and roots are used to make the pickle *wasabi-zuke*.

Wasabi has been so revered in Japan that throughout its history retired shōguns, or emperors, were given plantations to tend in retirement.

Young wasabi leaves can also be eaten and have a mild taste, which is more gentle on the tongue than the roots.

How do I grow it?

If you lack streams of fresh, flowing water in your garden, just grow wasabi in moist soil in the shade. Roots grow best in areas where conditions are cool in autumn and spring. Plants will also flourish in a large pot of loam-based compost, fed in spring with slow-release general fertilizer and kept constantly moist. Young roots have the best flavour, so divide up healthy plants every 2 years in early spring, and grow on in an unheated greenhouse or cold frame, before planting out in late spring the following year. Alternatively, propagate by detaching offsets from well-established plants in spring and replant.

The knobbly roots must be stripped of their lower leaf stems and sideroots, before being peeled and grated.

Quick guide

Plant in spring in situ or anytime when grown in containers

Minimum -5°C (23°F) to maximum 25°C (77°F)

Grow in full or part-shade, in damp, moist, humus-rich soil

Water extensively; never let the soil dry out

Plants grow up to 40cm (16in) high and wide

Harvest roots as needed and use immediately

Step-by-step growing ≫

Step-by-step growing

Buy container-raised plants to start growing wasabi; afterwards you can maintain your collection with offsets and plantlets from harvested roots. Protect from damage by slugs and cabbage caterpillars.

When to grow and harvest

Plant out after the last frosts. Harvest leaves and flowers as they appear and rhizomes as needed.

	early winter	late winter	early spring	late spring	early summer	late summer	early autumn	late autumn
plant				●	●			
harvest	●	●	●	●	●	●	●	●

① Grow on and prep the soil

Transplant container-raised plants into 9cm (3½in) pots of loam-based compost and grow on in a shady spot, potting on as they grow, until the danger of frost has passed. Wasabi grows best when its feet are in clean, nutrient-rich, running water. It will grow in a damp, shady position in the garden or at the edge of a pond, athough the roots will rot if the soil is too wet. Improve the drainage, structure, and nutrient levels of the soil ahead of planting by digging in plenty of well-rotted organic matter; leave the soil to settle.

Mail-order plants often arrive wrapped in damp hessian. Transplant them immediately into individual pots.

② Plant out

Water the plants in their containers and allow them to drain. Dig a hole in the ground slightly larger than the pot, ease the plant from the pot, and gently tease out the roots. Water the bottom of the hole if the soil is dry. Once the water has drained away, plant the wasabi so the compost surface is just above the level of the surrounding soil. Firm in the soil and water thoroughly. If growing in containers, plant in loam-based compost mixed with a few handfuls of grit to improve drainage.

Give plants a good soak before planting out, to keep them growing well until the roots get established.

③ Aftercare

Feed in spring with slow-release general fertilizer and keep plants well-watered. A mulch of compost or gravel will help lock in moisture. Gravel also works as a deterrent to slugs and snails, and there are numerous other environmentally friendly ways to combat them: encourage predators like ground beetles, frogs, toads, and thrushes; use nematodes; place copper tape round pots; or douse plants with garlic spray. Cabbage caterpillars also find the leaves tasty as the plant is in the Brassica family. Protect with horticultural fleece or fine mesh netting placed over a frame of stakes; this allows a gap between the net and leaves, so the adult insects cannot reach them to lay eggs.

If temperatures get too high in summer plants may die back, but once the weather cools they will produce another flush of leaves.

④ Winter care and harvest

Remove and compost the leaves when they die back in autumn and protect from cold weather over winter by covering with horticultural fleece, or a layer of bracken or straw. It takes about 24 months for the rhizomes to reach harvestable size. Carefully dig up the plant, harvest the main root and leaves, then tease the small offsets or plantlets apart and replant. The whole plant is edible so eat the leaf stems, leaves, and flowers too.

Wasabi roots need 2 years or more for the flavour to mature.

Cook's tips

Keep fresh

Store roots in the fridge, wrapped in moistened paper towel. Rinse with cold water every few days and they will last up to a month.

How to eat

Young leaves can be eaten raw or sautéed. Grate the roots for pastes and as a flavouring. Roots reach maximum heat 5 minutes after grating; the heat starts to decline after 20 minutes.

- Add the paste to a hollandaise sauce and serve with poached, grilled, or roasted salmon. The sauce also goes well with pan-fried steak.
- Grate to add flavour to soups and noodles, in sashimi and sushi, and on seafood.
- Wasabi paste gives a special twist to devilled eggs.
- Mix grated root with soy sauce and sesame oil in a marinade for chicken.
- Use the leaves and flowers as an alternative to watercress or rocket in salads.

How to preserve

Wasabi root lasts up to a year if made into a paste and kept in the fridge. Try pickling the leaves and flowers.

{ **Level 2** *moderate* }

Japanese hardy ginger

Zingiber mioga

If you are a fan of ginger and would like to grow your own, but don't live in a tropical climate, try cultivating this closely related, cold-tolerant species. Unlike conventional root ginger, it is the stems and peculiar flower buds of this variety that are harvested.

What is it?

Exotic in appearance yet extremely hardy, *Zingiber mioga* is a tall, herbaceous perennial plant, found in the wild in parts of China, northern Vietnam, South Korea, and Japan, where it grows on shady slopes and mountain valleys among mixed and deciduous woodland. The short-lived, orchid-like flowers appear in midsummer at soil level or just peeping out from the soil. The plant is deeply rooted in Japanese culture, where annual *myoga matsuri* festivals are held to celebrate the mythology and folklore associated with the plant.

Of the more than 20,000 ancient family crests in Japan, one of the top 10 most common heraldic devices depicts two myoga flower buds facing each other.

The species has fresh green leaves and there are variegated cultivars available.

How do I grow it?

Plants are grown from rhizomes (underground stems similar to roots and tubers) planted in spring. You should only need to buy rhizomes once as these perennial plants will sprout again each spring after dying back in autumn, and you can refresh and expand your stock by dividing established plants or propagating from sections of new rhizomes. As a woodland plant, *Zingiber mioga* will thrive in part-shade and prefers a humus-rich, moisture-retentive yet well-draining soil. Plants grow well in large containers and the attractive foliage and fascinating flowers make it an appealing plant for balconies and small courtyard gardens. Although it is the hardiest member of the ginger family, plants benefit from a thick mulch in autumn as protection against winter chills.

The pinkish flower buds are known as *myoga no ko* or "children of myoga" in Japan and used as a spicy garnish.

Quick guide

Plant in spring once the danger of frost has passed

Minimum -23°C (-9°F) to maximum 28°C (82°F)

Grow in sun or part-shade in organic-rich soil

Water frequently to keep plants and soil constantly moist, but avoid waterlogging

Plants grow up to 1m (3ft) in height and spread to 1.5 m (5ft)

Harvest shoots in spring and flower buds in summer

Step-by-step growing »

Step-by-step growing

Japanese hardy ginger can be grown from rhizomes or container-raised plants available from specialist nurseries. They will thrive in a rich, free-draining, slightly acidic soil that doesn't get waterlogged in winter.

When to grow and harvest

This hardy ginger can be planted outdoors from late winter. Harvest new shoots in spring and flower buds in summer.

	early winter	late winter	early spring	late spring	early summer	late summer	early autumn	late autumn
plant		●	●					
harvest			●	●		●		

1 Plant out

Dig in plenty of organic matter, and leave the soil to settle, before planting. Plant container-raised plants so that the soil is at the same level as the compost. In heavier soils prone to waterlogging, add a 2cm (¾in) layer of gravel at the base of the planting hole as a precaution. Plant rhizomes with a 3cm (1¼in) layer of soil above them. Space plants 30–40cm (12–16in) apart. Japanese ginger is a vigorous grower and, once established, just a few plants will provide a plentiful harvest, so there should be no need to plant multiple rows.

Plant the bare-rooted rhizomes so that the tapered ends, from which new shoots emerge, are pointing upwards.

2 Growing in containers

Japanese ginger also does well in pots. Grow in free-draining, bark-based compost with 20 per cent chopped bark, or John Innes No.3 with 30 per cent added horticultural grit, and feed every 2 weeks with a general liquid fertilizer.

If temperatures are set to drop below -10°C (14°F), move container-grown plants to a sheltered spot or under cover.

Japanese ginger is a woodland plant and likes to grow in soil enriched with leaf mould and bark.

❸ Aftercare

Keep plants constantly moist, but never waterlogged. Protect young plants and new spring growth from slugs and snails, using any number of environmentally friendly methods, such as organic traps, nematodes, garlic spray, and copper tape around containers.

Unless plants are growing in a woodland border where there is natural leaf fall, Japanese ginger benefits greatly from a thick mulch of leaf mould applied in spring and autumn, and also for winter protection.

Propagate in spring by dividing established clumps as they start into growth, or replanting 15-20cm (6-8in) sections of rhizome taken from robust plants.

❹ Harvest

Wait until plants have had a year to establish themselves before harvesting. Cut a few young shoots from each plant when less than 40cm (16in) long. Look out for flowers from midsummer. Pick when they are still tight buds, but leave a few for their spectacular blooms.

Flowers form at the plant base and emerge out of the soil.

Cook's tips

Keep fresh

Stems and flower buds keep for 10 days in the fridge, wrapped in kitchen towel.

How to eat

Chopped flower buds and shoots are used raw as a garnish for many Asian dishes, especially sashimi and sushi. They can also be cooked whole or sliced, and added as a flavouring for stir-fries and stews.

- Scatter sliced shoots and chopped buds over miso soup and soba noodles.
- Skewer buds between cubes of marinated meat or tofu and cook on the barbecue.
- Chop the buds in half and fry in tempura batter; great with seafood tempura.
- The flavour goes particularly well with aubergine: try sprinkling over chunks roasted with soy and honey.
- Try using the shoots in place of lemongrass.

How to preserve

Make a quick pickle by boiling the buds for 1 minute in rice or cider vinegar mixed with sugar. Keeps for up to a week in the fridge.

Tea
Level 2
moderate

Camellia sinensis

Most of the world's tea is made in China and India, and you might imagine the leaves come from some exotic plant. However, the tea plant is in fact a species of camellia, a type of evergreen shrub grown in the West for its beautiful flowers for at least 200 years.

What is it?

Camellia sinensis is a long-lived shrub native to East Asia, where it is found growing in the wild in acidic soil in woodland. The young leaves and leaf buds of commercially grown shrubs are harvested and processed to make tea. There are "small leaf" and "large leaf" varieties; the latter not only have larger leaves and flowers, but the leaves are more widely spaced and they have greater vigour. The flowers burst into bloom in late summer and autumn and can also be added to the teapot.

When to grow and harvest
Plant in late autumn, late winter, or early spring. Harvest leaf tips in spring and flowers in autumn.

	early winter	late winter	early spring	late spring	early summer	late summer	early autumn	late autumn
plant		●	●					●
harvest			●	●			●	●

How do I grow it?

Grow from container-raised shrubs planted out in acidic soil in a partly shaded, sheltered location. Protect from frost, cold winds, and sun scorch. For the first few winters, cover young plants with horticultural fleece, or move potted plants to a cool greenhouse or conservatory with good air circulation. Water with rainwater, which is slightly acidic; use tap water only in emergencies.

The dainty white flowers produce a mass of prominent golden stamens and look especially attractive against the foil of glossy foliage.

① Plant out

If planting a number of specimens leave 90cm (35in) between each plant. Water plants with rainwater and allow to drain before planting. If the soil is dry, water the bottom of the hole and scatter root-boosting mycorrhizal fungi around the base. Plant so the compost surface is level with the surrounding soil. In alkaline areas, grow in containers of ericaceous compost with 20 per cent small-grade chipped bark added for drainage.

② Aftercare and pruning

Mulch in spring with an acidic pine needle mulch, and feed with ericaceous fertilizer at the same time. Water until established and then in drought. After the frosts, while the plant is dormant, cut back last year's growth by one third or a half to just above a leaf. The new shoots will produce more sideshoots and leaves. Do this annually to create a compact, productive bush. To enjoy the flowers, prune as above for the first 3 years, then allow to grow naturally.

③ Harvest

Do not overpick in the early years; just take a few leaves from each shrub until they are established and growing strongly. After that, pick all you like. Traditionally, the uppermost pair of leaves and leaf bud at the tip of each stem are picked. Older leaves can also be used to make tea, but the flavour is bitter and quite different to the young, tender shoots. Pick the flowers when they have opened fully but aren't yet going over.

Quick guide

Sow under cover in spring then plant out in warmer weather, or grow on under cover

Minimum 10°C (50°F) to maximum 30°C (86°F)

Grow on a sunny, sheltered site in free-draining soil

Keep moist but avoid waterlogging

Plants grow up to 60cm (24in) in both height and spread

Harvest leaves after flowering, once plants are well established

Sweetleaf

Level 2 moderate

Stevia rebaudiana

The leaves of *Stevia rebaudiana* are many times sweeter than sugar, yet calorie-free, and are used commercially as a sugar substitute. Grow your own plants at home and you can use the fresh leaves to enjoy a sweet hit without the guilt.

What is it?

This tender perennial of the daisy family, with attractive foliage and tiny white flowers, is native to Brazil and Paraguay, where the leaves are traditionally used as a treatment for colic, stomach problems, and even as a contraceptive. In commercial processing, the leaves are steeped in water, filtered, purified, and dried, to produce crystallized stevia extract. But home gardeners can simply harvest the leaves after flowering and use fresh or dried.

When to grow and harvest

Sow in spring, transplanting outdoors or growing on indoors. Harvest leaves after plants have flowered.

	early winter	late winter	early spring	late spring	early summer	late summer	early autumn	late autumn
sow indoors		•	•					
plant out				•	•			
harvest					•	•	•	

How do I grow it?

Sow from seed or buy plants from a specialist nursery. Although not hardy, sweetleaf can be grown in cooler climates as an indoor or greenhouse perennial, or an annual in borders or containers. Grow in a sunny position in free-draining soil, but keep it moist. Feed to encourage healthy growth and pinch out sideshoots so the plant becomes a bush rather than a leafy stick.

Grow sweetleaf outdoors as a perennial where temperatures remain above 10°C (50°F), or as an annual plant in cooler climates.

 ## 1 Sow indoors

In spring, sow indoors in trays or modules on to the surface of moist seed compost, and cover with a fine layer of compost or vermiculite. Put in a propagator at 25–27°C (77–81°F) or leave in a warm place in a polythene bag to maintain humidity; seeds take 1 or 2 weeks to germinate. When seedlings are large enough to handle, prick them out into pots of multi-purpose compost.

2 Grow on or plant out

Transplant into larger pots before plants become pot-bound, and either continue to grow under cover as a container plant or in a greenhouse border, or plant outdoors where soil temperatures are at least 10°C (50°F), after first hardening off (see p.62). Choose a site in rich, moist, well-draining soil in full sun. Space rows 50–60cm (20–24in) apart, with 45cm (18in) between plants. Perennial plants often keep their leaves but some may fall due to low light.

3 Aftercare and harvest

Pinch out the growing tips to encourage branching and to increase leaf production. Feed with a general fertilizer every 2 weeks when in growth, and water when the compost surface is dry. Control slugs with environmentally friendly pellets and traps, or biological controls, and encourage natural predators. Cut back to 2.5cm (1in) in spring to encourage growth. Once established, harvest a proportion of leaves from each plant as required.

Meadowsweet

Filipendula ulmaria

Level 1 easy

A hardy, moisture-loving plant, meadowsweet bears a succession of edible, frothy, white plumes from late spring to the first frosts. The flowers have a strong flavour, perhaps best described as marzipan with a metallic tang, while the leaves contain an aspirin-like compound and are often used in pain-relieving herbal remedies.

Quick guide

Plant in spring to allow a full growing season for plants to establish

Minimum -20°C (-4°F) to maximum 25°C (77°F)

Grow in sun or part shade in damp or boggy conditions

Keep well watered, especially if growing in containers

Reaches 1.2m (4ft) high with a spread of 60cm (2ft)

Harvest leaves before flowers appear, and pick flowers before they start to fade

What is it?

Meadowsweet is a compact, clump-forming, herbaceous perennial whose leaves and stems die back in winter, with new shoots appearing in the spring. It is found in damp and boggy soils, near water courses and wet woodlands, throughout Europe and West Asia. The buds, blossoms, seeds, and leaves are all edible. The flowers were once used to flavour mead, while the smell of the leaves is similar to cucumber.

When to grow and harvest
Plant out container-raised plants in early spring and the blooms should be ready for picking by early summer.

	early winter	late winter	early spring	late spring	early summer	late summer	early autumn	late autumn
plant			•	•	•			
harvest					•	•	•	

How do I grow it?

Meadowsweet is best grown from young plants bought from a garden centre or nursery in spring. All it needs for a happy life is wet ground and sunshine. The cultivars 'Aurea', with bright yellow leaves in spring fading to light green by midsummer, and 'Variegata', whose leaves have yellow splashes and margins, make fine feature plants for containers.

1 Plant out

Improve the soil by digging in well-rotted organic matter. Water the plant in its container and allow to drain. Dig a hole slightly larger than the container, water the bottom of the hole, and then scatter over a root-booster of mycorrhizal fungi when the water drains off. Remove the plant from its pot and gently tease out the roots. Position it in the hole and backfill with compost until level with the soil surface. Water in thoroughly.

Meadowsweet thrives in wet soil. If growing in a container, use a loam-based compost such as John Innes No.3.

② Aftercare

To avoid the soil drying out, mulch around the plant with a 3cm (1¼in) layer of well-rotted organic matter in spring, and water constantly during the growing season. Place container-grown plants in part shade to avoid leaf scorch and so that the compost dries out slowly. If soil conditions are too dry, the leaves will shrivel and suffer from powdery mildew, a whitish fungus that appears on the leaf surfaces. Feed with a slow-release general fertilizer in spring.

③ Harvest and winter care

Pick flower heads when most of the flowers have opened and before they start to fade. Pick leaves young and fresh, but not too many from one plant. Cut back plants in autumn and keep weed free through the winter. Move container plants into a sheltered position under a tree, at the base of a sheltered wall, or into a garage or shed, to protect from frost. Just before growth starts again in spring, transplant into a pot one size larger.

FRUIT

Quick guide

Plant in spring once the danger of frost has passed

Minimum -12°C (10°F) to maximum 45°C (113°F)

Needs a sheltered, sunny position in rich, free-draining soil

Keep vines well watered during the growing season

Can climb as far as 9m (28ft)

Harvest from summer to autumn when the fruits are ripe

Kiwiberry

Level 3 advanced

Actinidia arguta

The size of a large grape, kiwiberries are the diminutive cousins of the fuzzy brown kiwi fruit common to supermarkets. No need to peel – these sweet, moreish berries can be enjoyed plucked straight off the rapidly growing vines.

What is it?

The kiwiberry is a vigorous, hardy, perennial climbing plant native to more northerly parts of East Asia. Most varieties have male and female flowers on different plants, which means at least one plant of each sex is needed to produce fruit. Male plants must be growing around 60cm (24in) from females to pollinate successfully, though a single male can pollinate several females. The job of transferring pollen can be left to insects, or you can pollinate by hand with a paintbrush.

The kiwiberry vine has attractively coloured red stems and large, heart-shaped leaves.

When to grow and harvest

Plants produce fruit 3 to 4 years after planting. Prune regularly, and harvest throughout summer and autumn.

	early winter	late winter	early spring	late spring	early summer	late summer	early autumn	late autumn
plant				•				
harvest					•	•	•	•

How do I grow it?

Kiwiberries can be grown without shelter in warm climates. In cooler areas young shoots can be damaged by frost in spring, so protect with horticultural fleece or old net curtains. Fruits need a long growing season to ripen and develop best against a pergola or sunny wall, with the stems supported by sturdy, free-standing galvanized wires set 30cm (12in) apart.

1 Planting and care

Buy container-raised plants in spring and plant outdoors about 30cm (12in) from the base of a wall or pergola and 3-4.5m (10-15ft) apart. Water thoroughly after planting and mulch with well-rotted organic matter. In late winter, mulch around the base of the plant with well-rotted manure. Apply slow release, general-purpose fertilizer around the base in spring, as growth starts. Keep moist during the growing season.

2 Initial training

After planting, cut back the main stem to 30cm (12in). Tie the new leading shoot to a cane attached vertically to horizontal wires. Tie in a pair of parallel sideshoots along each wire to form the main arms of the vine. Let laterals (sideshoots from main stems) grow out from these arms at roughly 50cm (20in) intervals and pinch out the tips when they produce 5 leaves. If growing up a pergola, allow one main stem to reach the top, then fan out sideshoots.

3 Aftercare and harvest

The following winter, cut existing laterals back to 3 or 4 buds beyond the last fruited stems. Thereafter, cut back each year about one quarter to one third of the oldest lateral stems to a single bud. Vines also need summer pruning to keep under control: pinch out any sideshoots growing from the laterals and main arms. Once the fruit has formed, pinch back the laterals, leaving 4 or 5 leaves beyond the maturing fruit. Harvest when fruits soften slightly, but are still firm.

Finger lime

Level 3 advanced

Citrus australasica

The finger lime is a remarkable plant. Open up its finger-like fruit and tiny pearls with the taste of lime and grapefruit burst out under the pressure. Widely used to garnish seafood, the pearls have the exquisite texture of caviar and "pop" in the mouth.

What is it?

As its latin name *Citrus australasica* suggests, the finger lime is a native of Australia, where it thrives as a thorny understory plant in the rainforests of Queensland and New South Wales. Fruits can grow up to 12cm (4¾in) long and usually have green-yellow skin and pulp, but there is a naturally occurring red-fleshed form, *Citrus australasica* var. *sanguinea*, and lots of colourful cultivars, too. When ripe, the fruit feel plump and detach easily from the plant – there will be plenty of picking to do!

In spring, pinch off the ends of young shoots with finger and thumb to encourage branching, but watch out for the thorns.

When to grow and harvest

Finger lime is in active growth in spring and summer, but can produce fruits throughout the year.

	early winter	late winter	early spring	late spring	early summer	late summer	early autumn	late autumn
plant				●	●			
move outdoors					●			
move indoors							●	
harvest	●	●	●	●	●	●	●	●

How do I grow it?

In cool climates, finger limes are best grown in containers so they can be moved outdoors when it's warm enough and brought back in under cover when it's not. Find them a warm, sheltered, sunny position in summer and bring indoors well before the first frosts. Overwinter plants in a moderately warm, bright, draught-free place. Repot in spring before they become pot-bound.

1 Plant and move outdoors

From late spring, plant container-raised plants in pots of well-drained, gritty, acidic compost, such as a citrus compost, or John Innes No.2 mixed with 20 per cent sharp sand or horticultural grit. Move plants outdoors after the last frosts, placing them first in shade and moving them into the sun over several days to avoid scorching the leaves. Plants stop growing above 35°C (95°F), indoors and out, so ventilate as required.

② Summer care

In summer, water from above with tepid water, thoroughly soaking the compost, but not leaving it waterlogged; tap water is fine if it's not artificially softened. Feed weekly with summer citrus feed and spray with soft soap against red spider mite and mealy bug. Move indoors before the first frosts into a spot with constant temperatures, away from dry air and with maximum light, ideally at 10°C (50°F) or more. Mist plants growing indoors regularly to maintain humidity.

③ Winter care and harvest

When watering in winter, err on the dry side; overwatering in winter is a common cause of death. Feed with a winter citrus feed according to the manufacturer's instructions. In early spring, repot when needed into a pot one size larger. In the years they are not repotted, remove the top 5cm (2in) of old compost in late spring and replace with fresh compost. Leave fruit hanging on the tree until needed. Fruit is ripe if it feels full enough to burst and comes off the plant easily.

The deep red berries ripen into autumn and are used to make a traditional liqueur in southern Chile.

{Level 2 moderate} Chilean guava

Ugni molinae

This pretty, compact shrub makes an attractive, ornamental, and edible plant that is suitable for the small garden. The aromatic fruits are the size of blackcurrants, but taste like wild strawberries and bubblegum. It really should be more widely grown.

What is it?

This hardy evergreen shrub was introduced to European and North American gardeners by the plant hunter William Lobb in 1844, who found it growing in Chile, both wild in woodland and scrub, and in private gardens as a fruit bush for desserts. It was hoped the shrubs would become equally popular in the northern hemisphere. Trials were undertaken and prizes offered in competitions at horticultural shows, but the plant never caught on. Perhaps its moment of glory is now!

Chilean guava was said to have been Queen Victoria's favourite fruit because the berries have little crowns.

The light pink flowers are sweetly scented and blossom from late spring.

How do I grow it?

Chilean guava needs shelter, sunshine, and moisture to flourish, but given all that it then requires little in the way of aftercare. The shrubs are suitable for hedging, even in small gardens, and specimens grow well in containers where their attractive, fragrant flowers can be closely appreciated. Plants need shelter from cold winds, which can scorch the leaves, and this will also help insect pollinators do their job. Unlike blueberries, Chilean guava thrives in both acidic and alkaline conditions, provided it is not shallow chalk.

Quick guide

Plant in spring so it has the whole growing season to establish

Minimum -10°C (14°F) to maximum 25°C (77°F)

Grow under shelter in full sun or part-shade, and acidic or alkaline, well-drained soil

Water often to keep the soil moist

Plants grow to 1.5m (5ft) in height and 1m (3ft) in spread

Pick the red fruits in late summer and early autumn

Step-by-step growing »

Step-by-step growing

Grow in a sunny site, planted out or in pots, and keep the soil or compost moist throughout the growing season. Provide winter protection in colder areas and exposed sites.

When to grow and harvest

Plant in spring or early summer and enjoy the berries from late summer to early autumn.

	early winter	late winter	early spring	late spring	early summer	late summer	early autumn	late autumn
plant			•	•	•			
harvest						•	•	

1 Plant out

Buy container-raised plants for planting out after the last frosts. Choose a position that will shelter the evergreen leaves from cold, drying winds, otherwise it will tolerate most well-drained soil types. Mature shrubs can reach an eventual spread of 1m (3ft), so bear this in mind for spacings if planting more than one. Water the plant in its container and allow to drain. Dig a hole in the ground slightly larger than the pot, ease the plant from the pot, and gently tease out the roots. Water the bottom of the hole if the soil is dry and, once the water has drained away, scatter root-boosting mycorrhizal fungi around the base of the hole where they will come into contact with the roots. Plant the shrub so the compost surface is at the level of the surrounding soil and firm in. Water thoroughly and mulch with well-rotted organic matter or forest bark.

Chilean guava also grows very well in a large container. For a growing medium, use John Innes No.3 compost or similar, mixed with 20 per cent well-rotted organic matter or general compost. Place the containers in a sunny, sheltered position where you, and the insects, can enjoy the intoxicating scent of the flowers.

If growing in a pot, plant a single specimen in a container 35cm (14in) in diameter with a volume of 20 litres, and pot on to a larger size as required.

35cm (14in)

Give the container-raised shrubs a thorough soak in their pots before planting out, so that they keep growing strongly while the roots are getting established.

③ Aftercare and pruning

Mulch in spring when the soil is damp to conserve moisture and suppress weeds. If growing in pots, keep plants moist and feed in spring with slow-release general fertilizer. Repot into larger containers in late winter or early spring if they start to look pot-bound. If their site is affected by cold winds, protect over winter with horticultural fleece.

Prune in spring after the frosts. Remove dead, dying, or crossing branches and any that are badly placed, weak, or damaged. Give container plants a more general trim to keep them manageable.

The bell-like flowers have an understated appearance but a strong fragrance.

④ Harvest

Pick the cranberry-sized berries from late summer when they have taken on a deep red colour. Harvest on a dry day and try a few first to check for ripeness. You may need to pick over the plant several times to gather the whole crop.

Ripe berries are slightly soft to the touch.

Cook's tips

Keep fresh

Store dry, undamaged, berries in a sealed plastic bag, or container lined with kitchen roll, in the fridge for up to a week.

How to eat

The fruits can be used in place of cranberries and blueberries in most recipes.

- Add to any fruit salad or layer in a Rumtopf.
- Make a compote by simmering the berries with a little water and sugar until they start to release their juices.
- Turn into a Chilean guava pie for pudding.
- Use in your favourite muffin or cupcake recipe instead of other fresh berries.
- Stir into the mix of a lemon polenta cake or add a layer to the base of a cake tin for an upside-down treat.
- Replaces cranberries in a sauce for roast lamb or turkey.

How to preserve

Cook with quince and reduce down to make the traditional Chilean preserve known as *murta con membrillo*. The fruits also make excellent jams and jellies.

Honeyberry

Level 1 *easy*

Lonicera caerulea varieties

This easy-to-grow shrub in the honeysuckle family produces unusually shaped, frosted-blue berries that taste like blueberry, blackberry, and raspberry rolled into one. The fruits contain high levels of vitamin C and potassium, and their antioxidant content is reported to be three times higher than that of blueberries.

Quick guide

Plant container-raised shrubs in spring

Minimum -40°C (-40°F) to maximum 30°C (86°F)

Grow in full sun, ideally in soil rich in organic matter and free draining

Water frequently to keep the soil moist

Plants grow up to 1.2m (4ft) in height and spread

Harvest ripe fruits from late spring to early summer

What is it?

Honeyberry is an extremely hardy shrub that grows well in most soils. Two or more plants of different varieties are needed to produce a good crop. Cultivars of *Lonicera caerulea* var. *edulis* offer some of the best eating varieties: 'Atut' is a good pollinator for 'Duet'. Another superior eating variety is *Lonicera caerulea* var. *kamtschatica*, which includes cultivars 'Larisa' and 'Rebecca' for heavy cropping and sweet flavour, and 'Maries' for a very compact habit, suitable for small gardens and containers.

When to grow and harvest

Plant shrubs in spring and expect your first harvest 2 years later in late spring and early summer.

	early winter	late winter	early spring	late spring	early summer	late summer	early autumn	late autumn
plant			●	●				
harvest				●	●			

How do I grow it?

Best grown from container-raised plants, honeyberry thrives in both acid and alkaline soils, making it a useful alternative to blueberry in non-acid soil. Its compact size and ability to grow in pots make it ideal for a small garden.

Honeyberry plants grow attractive, sea-green foliage, and small, pale yellow flowers that appear from very late winter to early spring.

① Planting and aftercare

Plant in spring after the last frost, in free-draining soil enriched with garden compost or well-rotted manure. Water well after planting, and mulch with well-rotted organic matter or forest bark. Keep the soil moist and apply a balanced fertilizer every spring. Net the plants or grow in a fruit cage to protect berries from birds. Plants can also be grown in pots of loam-based compost, and potted on into larger containers each year.

Cook's tips

Keep fresh
Store berries in the fridge in a sealed container lined with paper towels.

How to eat
Eat raw or use in cooking instead of blueberries.

- Make a sauce for roast pork, venison, or duck.
- Chop into a fruity salsa for veggie burgers, with onion, chilli, coriander, and lime juice.
- Simmer with a little water to make a compote for pancakes.

How to preserve
Berries can be frozen or turned into jam, or try pickling in a sweetened vinegar flavoured with rosemary sprigs.

② Pollination and harvest

Plants growing in a warm, sunny site, sheltered from the wind, tend to be good croppers as insect pollinators are more likely to be active early in the season, when the shrubs are in flower. You can also pollinate by hand, using a soft brush to transfer pollen from the flowers of one variety to another. Harvest fruits when the ripe berries have turned blue with a whitish bloom, and the flesh is dark purple.

③ Pruning

Plants can take up to 2 years to begin fruiting. Once they've started bearing berries, give shrubs a light annual pruning from early to midsummer, after fruiting. Remove dead, diseased, dying, crossing, and rubbing branches, and weak or damaged shoots and stems. Thin out overcrowded shoots, cutting several back to the base to allow young, vigorous regrowth. Remove the tips of young shoots to encourage the growth of flowering sideshoots.

Quick guide

Plant out after the last frosts and when the soil has warmed

Minimum -15°C (5°F) to maximum 30°C (86°F)

Grow in sun or dappled shade, in moisture-retentive soil or compost

Keep well watered throughout the growing season

Hardy fuchsias grow up to 2m (6½ft) high and wide; half-hardy are smaller

Harvest berries when they are intensely coloured

Fuchsia berry

Level 2 moderate

Fuchsia species and cultivars

While fuchsias are widely grown for their attractive flowers, most growers are yet to discover the appeal of their berries. All types bear edible berries, but size and flavour vary greatly. *Fuchsia* 'Genii' and *F. magellanica* produce superior-tasting berries, and the cultivar 'Fuchsiaberry' has been specially selected for its fruits.

What is it?

Native to mountainous parts of New Zealand and Central and South America, fuchsias are flowering shrubs ranging in cold-tolerance from fully hardy to frost tender. Depending on variety, flowers bloom from mid-spring to mid-autumn, followed by berries with a texture similar to soft grapes and ranging in flavour from intensely sweet to slightly bitter, with notes of fig, kiwi, pomegranate, and spice.

When to grow and harvest

Plant in spring and harvest the ripe fruits from midsummer to late autumn, depending on variety.

	early winter	late winter	early spring	late spring	early summer	late summer	early autumn	late autumn
plant			●	●	●			
harvest					●	●	●	●

Fuchsia magellanica bears an abundance of flowers throughout summer, followed by purple fruits with a peppery, grape-like taste.

How do I grow it?

Fuchsias will grow in almost any soil, but prefer shelter from cold winds and a relatively sunny spot, though they like shade during the hottest part of the day. *Fuchsia magellanica* and *F.* 'Genii' are more hardy than *F.* 'Fuchsiaberry', but all will require protection over winter. 'Genii' and 'Fuchsiaberry' are compact varities suited to growing in large containers.

1 Planting

Buy container-raised plants for planting out. Hardy types can be planted immediately. Half-hardy fuchsias should be potted on indoors and, when there is no further risk of frost, acclimatized to outdoor conditions by placing them in a cloche or cold frame and gradually increasing ventilation, first during the day and then also at night. Once hardened off, transplant to their final positions. Several plants together will produce heavier crops.

Cook's tips

Keep fresh
Store unblemished berries in a sealed container in the fridge or cool pantry.

How to eat
Fuchsia berries can be used as a substitute for cherries, grapes, and blueberries in most recipes.

- Cook gently with sugar and a little water to make a compote.
- Bake in a sweet eggy batter for clafoutis.
- Add to the roasting pan for chicken or game birds.

How to preserve
Berries can be frozen, made into jam, or stored fresh under sugar syrup – try flavouring the syrup with your favourite spirit.

2 Aftercare and harvest

Increase watering once the fuchsia plants start to grow in late spring. Feed with liquid general fertilizer to encourage growth until the plants are established. Then, switch to a high-potash feed, such as dilute liquid tomato fertilizer, to promote flowering and fruiting. As plants grow, nip out the shoot tips from the main stems to encourage branching and further flower production. Harvest fruits when they are fully coloured and slightly soft to the touch.

3 Winter care

Half-hardy fuchsias need frost protection over winter. Store them in their pots in a cool, frost-free greenhouse, shed, or garage. Leave on as much foliage as space allows, for extra protection. In spring, cut back the main stems to within 5cm (2in) of the base, and spray with water to encourage regrowth. Hardy fuchsias can remain outside through the winter, and in mid-spring they should be cut back almost to ground level above a strong pair of buds.

{ Level 2 *moderate* }

Cape gooseberry

Physalis peruviana

For a fuss-free plant with architectural appeal and exotic-tasting fruit, look no further than the Cape gooseberry, whose sweet-sharp berries are borne prolifically throughout summer and autumn, concealed within their Chinese lanterns.

What is it?

Despite originating in Peru, the plant became known as the Cape gooseberry because it was first mass-cultivated by European farmers on the Cape of Good Hope in South Africa, who grew the fruits to make jam for export. Cape gooseberry is a perennial plant in the wild, but is grown as an annual in cooler climates as it needs protection from frost over the winter. Plants produce soft, heart-shaped leaves, delicate yellow-and-pink flowers, and bright orange fruits high in carotenes, potassium, and vitamin C.

The fruit has been given many common names in its travels round the world, including poha, husk cherry, Peruvian ground cherry, and goldenberry.

Berries grow enclosed in a balloon-like calyx that turns from green to pale beige.

How do I grow it?

The Cape gooseberry is a member of the same family of plants as tomatoes and can be grown in a similar way. Start plants off under cover in cooler areas and either transplant outdoors to a warm, sheltered spot in full sun, after the danger of frost has passed, or continue growing under cover in pots, growing bags, or moved to a border in a greenhouse or polytunnel. Plants also grow happily in large containers of multi-purpose compost in a sheltered spot. If you are growing them in a greenhouse, ventilate well on hot days and keep plants constantly moist. Fruits ripen from early summer and can be left on the plant until needed. Peak flavour is 2 to 3 weeks after ripening.

If frosts threaten late fruits they can be picked and ripened fully on a sunny windowsill.

Quick guide

Sow under cover in early spring, then plant out once there is no danger of frost

Minimum 5°C (41°F) to maximum 30°C (86°F)

Grow in light, free-draining soil in a warm spot

Water moderately and avoid waterlogging

Plants grow up to 90cm (35in) in both height and spread

Harvest when the husks turn papery and the fruits are golden

Step-by-step growing »

Step-by-step growing

For a bumper crop of beautiful golden fruits, grow Cape gooseberries in a warm position, water well but not excessively, and aid pollination by gently tapping the flowers.

When to grow and harvest
Sow seeds in spring, and plant out when all danger of frost has passed. Harvest the berries from summer to autumn.

	early winter	late winter	early spring	late spring	early summer	late summer	early autumn	late autumn
sow indoors			●					
plant out				●				
harvest					●	●	●	●

1 Sow indoors

Start plants off under cover in early spring. Thickly sow seeds approximately 6mm (¼in) deep in seed compost, such as John Innes No.1, in trays or modules. Place on a sunny windowsill or in a propagator set at a temperature of 18°C (64°F). Germination should take around 10–14 days. When the seedlings are large enough to handle, carefully transplant them individually into 7.5cm (3in) pots also filled with seed compost. Continue to grow plants on under cover, repotting into larger pots as needed.

Use a dibber to help you separate out the tiny seedlings and avoid damaging their delicate roots.

2 Plant out

Rake the soil of the planting location to a fine texture and enrich it by adding well-rotted organic matter, especially if growing on a chalky soil. Once all danger of frost has passed, acclimatize plants to outdoor conditions by placing them in a cloche or cold frame and gradually increasing ventilation, first during the day and then also at night. Water thoroughly in their pots before planting outdoors at the spacings below.

Young plants must be gradually exposed to the winds and colder temperatures outside.

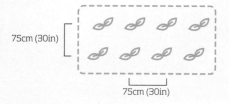

75cm (30in)

75cm (30in)

Space plants 75cm (30in) apart, leaving the same distance between rows.

③ Aftercare

Protect plants from strong winds with cloches or horticultural fleece until they are established. Pinch out the growing tips when plants are 30cm (12in) tall, to encourage branching and fruit formation. The stems are very lax and will need some form of support. Feed with a high-potash feed, such as dilute liquid tomato fertilizer, once the first flowers appear. Keep the soil moist but don't overwater, as this stimulates leafy growth at the expense of flowers. Tap or gently shake the flowers to aid pollination.

Support plants with string tied round a frame of stakes, or tie individually to canes.

④ Harvest and winter care

Harvest from early to midsummer when the berries are golden-yellow and fully ripe, discarding the inedible husks. Plants grown in pots can be brought under cover and kept somewhere cool but frost-free over winter. Plants in the ground can be also be lifted, transferred to pots, and stored over winter. Overwintered plants start fruiting earlier next year.

The husks turn brown and papery as the fruits ripen inside.

Cook's tips

Keep fresh
Perfect, unblemished berries will keep for several days stored in a sealed polythene bag in the fridge.

How to eat
The slightly tart fruits can be eaten raw or cooked in sweet or savoury dishes.

- Spread whipped cream over meringue and top with Cape gooseberries, apricot halves, and raspberries for a quick summer dessert.
- For an after-dinner treat, coat berries in melted dark chocolate and leave to dry.
- Combine with cooking apples for an autumn crumble.
- Add whole or halved to a salad of sweetcorn, cucumber, and coriander leaves.
- Mix in chopped berries to tomato salsa for a fruity twist – great with Mexican food.

How to preserve
Cape gooseberry makes an excellent jam and its slightly tart flavour works well in chutneys. Fruits can also be preserved whole in a sugar-and-honey syrup.

Goji berry

Level 2 moderate

Lycium barbarum

A native of China, the goji berry has gained a global reputation as a superfood. Legend has it that the Chinese herbalist Li Qing Yuen consumed goji berries daily and lived to be 252 years old. However unlikely the legend, there is no denying that the fruits contain very high levels of vitamin C and antioxidants.

Quick guide

Plant container-raised shrubs in late summer or early autumn

Minimum -10°C (14°F) to maximum 30°C (86°F)

Grow in free-draining soil in a sheltered, sunny position

Water young plants in late spring and summer; established plants rarely need watering

Pruned plants rarely exceed 90cm (3ft) in height and spread

Harvest after 2 to 3 years, from late summer to the first frosts

What is it?

Goji berry is a deciduous shrub that bears small, trumpet-shaped, white or purple flowers from early spring to midsummer, followed by a prolific crop of shiny, oval, orange-red berries with a sweet-savoury flavour. Once established, plants are hardy and vigorous, producing many long, arching stems with a lax habit. Mature shrubs can tolerate wind and drought, as well as salt-laden air in coastal areas.

When to grow and harvest

Plant from late summer to autumn. Two to three years later, harvest from early to midsummer onwards.

	early winter	late winter	early spring	late spring	early summer	late summer	early autumn	late autumn
plant						●	●	
harvest					●	●	●	

Goji berries can be grown from seed, but it is simpler to buy container-raised plants and plant them out in your garden.

How do I grow it?

Goji berry can be grown from seed, but it is more practical to buy container-raised plants. Plants crop most heavily in well-drained soil in a sunny position, but tolerate partial shade. The lax stems benefit from being trained against trellis or on wires fixed to a wall. Goji can also be grown in large containers on a sunny patio or as a hedge trimmed in summer.

1 Planting and aftercare

Plant in late summer or autumn in free-draining soil enriched with garden compost, spacing plants 2m (6½ft) apart. Water in thoroughly and mulch around the base with well-rotted organic matter or forest bark. For the first winter, protect young plants with horticultural fleece. Feed in late spring with a slow-release general-purpose fertilizer. Water young plants from late spring to late summer until established.

 **Harvest**

Goji shrubs will take 2 to 3 years to produce their first crops, as flowers and fruit develop on the previous year's stems. Harvest berries from early summer until the first frosts. The fruits are only edible when they are red and fully ripe. Sometimes berries can turn black when they are handled. To avoid this, place an old sheet or soft bag beneath the fruits to catch them, and gently shake the plant.

3 Pruning

Prune lightly as the shrubs start into growth in early spring. Remove any dead, damaged, or badly placed shoots. Cut overlong stems back to a well-placed branch to keep the shrub within its allotted space, and remove some of the oldest wood at the base. Tangled, woody specimens can be rejuvenated in early spring by cutting back the whole plant to a low framework of branches close to the base. Cut back container-grown plants by up to half after fruiting.

{ **Level 1** easy }

Chokeberry

Aronia melanocarpa or A. x prunifolia

This ornamental but highly productive shrub is grown for its attractive flowers, richly coloured autumn foliage, and lustrous, deep purple – almost black – fruits. The berries contain very high levels of vitamin C and their antioxidant content is reported to be three times higher than that of blueberries.

Quick guide

Plant outdoors at any time

Minimum -40°C (-40°F) to maximum 30°C (86°F)

Grow in moist but well-drained soil in sun or partial shade

Water regularly to keep the soil constantly moist

Plants grow up to 1.5m (5ft) in height and spread

Harvest in autumn, when the berries are deep purple and fully ripe

What is it?

Chokeberry is an extremely hardy, deciduous shrub from eastern North America, where it grows in woodland clearings and scrub. Cropping is prolific in moist, peaty soil, but shrubs grow well on most soils, except for shallow chalk and waterlogged ground. The brilliant autumn foliage makes it an attractive hedging plant, and it is an excellent compact shrub for small gardens.

When to grow and harvest
Shrubs can be planted all year round. Harvest the fully ripe berries in autumn.

	early winter	late winter	early spring	late spring	early summer	late summer	early autumn	late autumn
plant	•	•	•	•	•	•	•	•
harvest							•	•

How do I grow it?
Container-raised specimens of this robust, versatile shrub are readily available to buy and can be planted outdoors at any time of year. Aftercare needs are minimal: give plants a good mulch in spring to help retain moisture; protect the developing berries from birds with netting; and, once plants are established, undertake a regime of simple pruning in late winter.

The dark, glossy leaves and hawthorn-like, white flowers are followed in mid-autumn by deep purple fruits similar to blackcurrants.

① Plant outdoors

Give the shrubs in their pots a good soak before planting. Dig a hole slightly larger than the pot, remove the plant from the pot, and gently tease out the roots. Water the bottom of the hole if the soil is dry, allow it to drain, and then scatter over root-boosting mycorrhizal fungi. Plant the shrub so that the container compost surface is level with the surrounding soil. Backfill and firm the soil around the stem, then water in thoroughly.

Cook's tips

Keep fresh
Seal in a container lined with kitchen towel and keep in the fridge for up to a week.

How to eat
Fruits are a little sour when raw and are best eaten cooked and sweetened.

- Use in place of blackcurrants in desserts and bakes.
- Serve a chokeberry relish with cooked or smoked salmon.
- Stir into meaty stews and bean chilli for a sweet-sour depth of flavour.

How to preserve
Surplus berries can be frozen, dried in a very low oven or dehydrator, or used to make jams and jellies.

2 Aftercare

After planting when the soil is still moist, and each spring thereafter, mulch with a thick layer of well-rotted organic matter or forest bark, leaving a small gap between the mulch and the stem so the mulch doesn't start to rot the stem. Each spring, feed with a slow-release fertilizer designed for acid-loving, flowering plants. Cover plants with fine netting in late summer to protect your crop from birds, or consider growing shrubs in a fruit cage.

3 Harvest and pruning

Pick fruits when they have ripened to a deep purple colour and glossy appearance. Grasp a cluster of berries and dislodge them all at once with a downward dragging movement.

Plants will need pruning in late winter after their second year of growth. Use secateurs to remove a third of the older stems at the base, which will encourage new, productive growth. You will also need to dig up any suckers to keep plants within their allotted space.

The orange fruits are more subtle in taste than the tropical versions found in supermarkets, but no less delicious.

Level 2 *moderate*

Hardy passion fruit

Passiflora caerulea

Passion flowers are among the most exotic blooms on earth and plants are often grown purely as ornamentals. *Passiflora caerulea*, whose beauty belies its robustness, produces tasty fruits that deserve to be more widely eaten.

> When Spanish missionaries first saw the flower in the wild, they perceived a symbolism in its floral parts that related to the passion of Jesus Christ.

What is it?

A perennial climber from southern Brazil, hardy passion fruit effortlessly scrambles with the aid of tendrils. Plants bear large, glossy green leaves divided into long-fingered lobes, followed in midsummer by flowers with blue-banded coronas. From these develop the bright orange fruits, which are roughly the size of hen's eggs and filled with masses of seeds surrounded by sweet-tasting pulp.

How do I grow it?

Cold-tolerant enough to be grown outside in temperate areas, hardy passion fruit may still be cut back by the cold in severe winters, and planting it in very free-draining soil – even builders' rubble – will increase the chances of survival. Give it a sheltered spot against a hot, sunny wall, and train the shoots up wires or trellis. Hardy passion fruit also grows happily in a large container in a sunny location. With its striking flowers followed by colourful fruit, it makes an highly ornamental addition to a border or boundary.

Spectacular blue-and-white flowers appear from midsummer to early autumn, and can be up to 10cm (4in) across.

Quick guide

Sow seed from early spring for planting out after the last frosts

Minimum -15°C (5°F) to maximum 30°C (86°F)

Grow by a sheltered, sunny wall in fertile, free-draining soil

Keep moist during the growing season, particularly if growing in containers

Can climb to around 15m (49ft) in warm conditions

Pick from midsummer when the fruit is ripe and golden

Step-by-step growing »

Step-by-step growing

Grow plants from seed, starting under cover in early spring, or buy container-raised plants for planting out after the last frosts. Grow against a wall or trellis in a sheltered position in sun or partial shade.

When to grow and harvest

Plant in spring, and harvest the fruit from midsummer onwards as it ripens.

	early winter	late winter	early spring	late spring	early summer	late summer	early autumn	late autumn
sow indoors			●	●	●			
plant out				●	●			
harvest					●	●	●	

1 Sow indoors

Sow seeds in individual pots or modules from early spring to early summer. Sow one seed per pot or module, inserting the seed 1cm (½in) deep in seed compost. Put the pots on a warm windowsill or in a propagator set to 19–24°C (66–77°F); germination can take up to 6 weeks. When the seedlings are large enough to handle, carefully transfer them to larger pots filled with multi-purpose compost. Continue to grow on under cover, repotting as they outgrow their containers. After the last frosts, acclimatize the plants to outdoor conditions by placing in a cloche or cold frame and gradually increasing ventilation, first during the day and then also at night.

Take care to avoid too much disturbance of the roots when potting on the seedlings.

2 Plant outdoors

When the weather is mild and the soil has warmed, transplant the young plants to their final positions in a sheltered site outdoors. Alternatively, you can buy and plant container-raised passion flowers. The procedure for planting is the same for indoor-sown plants. Water the pots thoroughly and allow to drain. Dig a hole slightly larger than the size of the pot, 60cm (24in) away from the wall or trellis. Ease the plant from the pot and gently tease out the roots. Water the bottom of the planting hole and allow the water to drain away, before sprinkling a handful of root-boosting mycorrhizal fungi. Plant so the compost is level with the surrounding soil, firm in, and water thoroughly.

Water both the plants in their pots and the base of the planting hole to help the roots establish.

Fruits turn from green to orange as they ripen.

③ Aftercare and harvest

Water new plants during dry weather, but only water mature plants if they show signs of stress. Feed with slow-release general fertilizer in spring. As new shoots develop, train them along wires or up a trellis. Harvest when fruits turn orange and soften. In autumn, after fruiting, prune out the shoots that have borne fruit, to encourage the growth of new shoots the following year. When the plant has filled its allotted space, give it a more general prune every spring to keep it under control. Mulch the base of the plant with a thick layer of well-rotted garden compost or bark chippings to retain moisture around the roots and protect against frost.

Growing in containers

Hardy passion fruit will thrive if grown in a large container in a warm location, such as a sunny patio. Use a free-draining, loam-based compost enriched with organic matter. As the plant grows, pot it on into a slightly larger container each spring, until the foliage covers the allotted space. Water container-grown plants regularly, but allow the compost surface almost to dry out before rewatering.

Cook's tips

Keep fresh
Hardy passion fruit is best eaten fresh, ripened on the vine. Fruit will last for 2 or 3 days in the fruit bowl.

How to eat
Fruits are at their peak of ripeness and flavour when the skin just starts to shrivel. The outer flesh is relatively bland and it is the inner seed-filled pulp that you want to eat.

- Add to smoothies.
- Make a sponge cake filling by mixing with sweetened mascarpone, or use to flavour a syrup for drizzling over polenta cake.
- Combine with papaya for a tropical pavlova topping.
- Spread over cream as a filling for meringue roulade.
- Make passion fruit liqueur with vodka and sugar syrup.

How to preserve
Cut the fruits in half, scoop out the pulp into an ice cube tray, then freeze. Once frozen, put the cubes in freezer bags for indefinite storage. Passion fruit also makes a superb jam partnered with apricots.

Level 1 easy

Oregon grape

Mahonia aquifolium

A familiar garden plant, the glossy, holly-like leaves and bright yellow flower clusters of the Oregon grape often spread through shady shrub borders. Blackbirds love their late summer berries, but few gardeners realise that they could be feasting on them too.

What is it?

Oregon grape is a hardy, low-growing shrub, which spreads through the soil via suckers and makes a great ground cover plant. As its name suggests, the shrub is native to western North America, where it forms part of the understory of plants in forests and woodland. The plump, dark blue berries are traditionally gathered by Native American people, who mix them with other fruits to sweeten their tart flavour. Shrubs were introduced to Europe in 1822 and have since become widely naturalized.

When to grow and harvest
Plants take a few years to establish and spread before producing a useful crop of berries.

	early winter	late winter	early spring	late spring	early summer	late summer	early autumn	late autumn
sow outdoors			•				•	•
plant outdoors			•	•			•	•
harvest						•	•	

The fragrant yellow flowers of the Oregon grape grow in small bunches and tend to start blossoming in early spring.

How do I grow it?

This tough shrub is widely available from garden centres and is easy to grow anywhere with some shade and well-drained soil. Container-raised plants are best planted in spring or autumn and kept well watered while they establish. It is also possible to grow it from seed, which is best sown in autumn as soon as it is ripe, in an outdoor seedbed or cold frame.

1 Sow seeds

Seeds can be obtained from the ripe berries and should be sown immediately. First remove the soft surrounding flesh of the berry, then plant the seeds 1cm (1/2in) deep into an outdoor seedbed, 15cm (6in) apart, or into pots of moist compost in a cold frame. Germination requires a period of cold weather and seedlings will not usually emerge until the following spring. If sowing dry seed in spring, refrigerate for 3 weeks before planting.

Cook's tips

Keep fresh
Store in a plastic container in the fridge for up to a week.

How to eat
Berries can be eaten raw, though their sharp flavour and large seeds will not delight everyone. They are often cooked first to remove the pulp from the seeds.

- Try raw berries with yogurt and honey, or on top of muesli.
- Cook with a little water for 10-15 minutes, then press through a sieve and use the juice as a base for desserts and preserves.

How to preserve
Make jelly, wine, ice cream, and sorbet from the juice.

2 Transplant and plant out

When seedlings emerge, transplant those raised in a seedbed into pots, and grow on all plants in a cold frame, through the growing season and over winter, for planting out next spring. Improve the soil at the planting site by working in plenty of well-rotted compost, then position the plant in a hole to the same depth as it was in its pot, firm the soil around it, and water in. Shrubs bought from a garden centre are planted in the same way, ideally in spring or autumn.

3 Aftercare and harvest

Generally, these tough shrubs need little attention once planted out, but water them well during any dry weather in their first summer while they establish their roots. Apply a spring mulch of compost on lighter soils prone to drying out. Older plants respond well to pruning where growth has become straggly or tired. Pick the ripe berries by catching them in a container as you gently run your fingers down the stem.

Quick guide

Sow indoors in autumn or late winter to early spring

Minimum -10°C (14°F) to maximum 30°C (86°F)

Grow in moderately fertile soil in a sunny or partially shady spot

Water occasionally, keeping the soil or compost moist

Plants grow up to 50cm (20in) in height and spread

Pick when fruits are plump

{ *Level 1 easy* }

White alpine strawberry

Fragaria vesca alba and cultivars

These white strawberries may look unreal, but in fact derive from a wild species. With a longer cropping season than regular strawberries, you'll be picking the dainty fruits right up to the first frosts.

What is it?

White alpine strawberry plants are smaller than the garden variety, don't send out runners, and can tolerate cooler conditions. While fruits are lacking in the protein "Fra a1" that gives most strawberries their red colour, they are no less sweet and juicy. Alpine strawberries have not been intensively hybridized and there are fewer cultivars to choose from; perhaps the best are 'White Delight', closest to the wild species, and the strongly flavoured 'Pineapple Crush'.

Alpine strawberries self-seed feely and you can increase your stock of plants by lifting and transplanting any seedlings.

When to grow and harvest

Sow in autumn, late winter, or spring and harvest from summer to autumn.

	early winter	late winter	early spring	late spring	early summer	late summer	early autumn	late autumn
sow indoors		●	●	●				●
plant out			●	●				●
harvest					●	●	●	

How do I grow it?

As low-growing evergreen plants, they make attractive edging for paths and an excellent choice for ground cover. Plants form compact clumps and thrive in containers, so you don't need a lot of garden space to grow them.

1 Sow indoors

Sow seeds in trays of firmed John Innes No.1 compost or sieved multi-purpose compost, in autumn or from midwinter until early spring. Gently press seeds into the surface and lightly cover with perlite or sharp sand. Keep moist but not wet. Place under glass at a temperature of 18-20°C (64-68°F) and move to a shady spot or cover with newspaper until germination, which can be slow. Keep autumn sowings in a cold frame over winter.

② Pot on and plant

Once seedlings have a pair of true leaves, transplant into small pots of multi-purpose or loam-based compost. Harden off for 2 weeks by keeping them outside during the day and inside at night, or in a cold frame with the lid ajar during the day. Once the danger of frost has passed, plant out in a warm, sheltered, sunny spot with 25-30cm (10-12in) between plants and rows. Water thoroughly and mulch with well-rotted organic matter or forest bark.

③ Aftercare and harvest

Boost plants with slow-release general fertilizer or with high-potash fertilizer in early spring to encourage flowering. You may need to assist pollination by transferring pollen between flowers using a paintbrush. The white berries are less appealing to birds, but cover plants with a net as a precaution. Harvest the ripe berries in late summer the first year, and midsummer to autumn thereafter. Replace plants in rotation every three years to keep them vigorous.

RESOURCES

Index

Suppliers

The Beth Chatto Gardens Nursery
Nursery of the world-famous gardens noted for growing unusual plants.
bethchatto.co.uk

Brookfield Plants
Specialist suppliers of hostas and daylilies.
brookfieldplants.co.uk

Burncoose Nurseries
Mail-order suppliers of unusual fruits, ostrich ferns, daylilies, and hostas.
burncoose.co.uk

Chiltern Seeds
Seed supplier specialising in unusual plants.
chilternseeds.co.uk

Crocus
Large mail-order supplier of seeds and plants.
crocus.co.uk

Harper & Debbage
Specialist nursery for fuchsia plants.
harperanddebbage.co.uk

Hayloft
For rare, unusual, and exciting plants and seeds.
hayloft-plants.co.uk

Isle of Wight Garlic Farm
For elephant garlic cloves and monobulbs.
thegarlicfarm.co.uk

Lubera
For edible dahlias and other unusual fruit and veg.
lubera.co.uk

Nicky's Nursery
Seed company selling favourite, rare, and unusual garden seed.
nickys-nursery.co.uk

Pennard Plants
For heritage and heirloom seeds and plants.
pennardplants.com

Plants of Distinction
Suppliers of new, unusual, and heritage edibles.
plantsofdistinction.co.uk

Pomona Fruits
Specialist suppliers of fruit trees and bushes.
pomonafruits.co.uk

Suttons
Established supplier of seeds and plants, specialising in fruit and veg and with a range of unusual edibles.
suttons.co.uk

Thompson & Morgan
Large, established seller of seeds and plants.
thompson-morgan.com

Tregothnan
Cornish tea grower and supplier of tea plants.
tregothnan.co.uk

Victoriana Nursery Gardens
Family-run nursery supplying unusual, exotic, and heritage fruit, veg, and herbs.
victoriananursery.co.uk

World Wonders Gardens
For weird and wonderful seeds and plants from around the world.
worldwondersgardens.co.uk

Picture credits

The publisher would like to thank the following for their kind permission to reproduce their photographs:

(Key: a-above; b-below/bottom; c-centre; f-far; l-left; r-right; t-top)

18 Alamy Stock Photo: Nick Kurzenko tl. **19 Alamy Stock Photo**: Garden World Images Ltd / Oscar D'arcy tl. **82 Dorling Kindersley**: Mark Winwood bl. **117 123RF.com**: Yotrak Butda / yotrak. **133 Dorling Kindersley**: Mark Winwood / RHS Wisley tl, Peter Anderson br. **143 iStockphoto.com**: sherjaca. **147 Alamy Stock Photo**: Photos Horticultural / Avalon. **166 iStockphoto.com**: bdspn. **195 Alamy Stock Photo**: Nick Kurzenko. **203 Alamy Stock Photo**: Garden World Images Ltd / Oscar D'arcy. **205 Dorling Kindersley**: Roger Smith.

Cover images: *Front*: **Alamy Stock Photo**: age fotostock br, Chuck Franklin bl; **Getty Images**: Joy Skipper cla, Michael Davis tc; **iStockphoto.com**: bonchan tr, cra, juliedeshaies bc; *Back*: **Alamy Stock Photo**: age fotostock br, Chuck Franklin bl; **Getty Images**: Joy Skipper cla, Michael Davis tc; **iStockphoto.com**: bonchan tr, cra, juliedeshaies bc; *Spine*: **Alamy Stock Photo**: Westend61 GmbH t; Background: **123RF. com**: kaspri

All other images
© Dorling Kindersley
For further information see:
www.dkimages.com

About the author

MATTHEW BIGGS

Having trained at the Royal Botanic Gardens, Kew, Matthew Biggs is affectionately known as "The People's Gardener". Writer, lecturer, and television presenter, he is the author of several books, including *RHS Great British Village Show* and *The Complete Book of Vegetables*. Matt is best known for being a regular panellist on BBC Radio 4's much-loved *Gardeners' Question Time*.

Acknowledgements

Author's acknowledgements

I would like to thank David Hall, Matthew Oliver at RHS Hyde Hall, Alexis Datta, and Jacqui Ruthven for their time, knowledge, and gardening skills, Mark Winwood for his photographic talents, Jo Whittingham and Jessica Biggs for their horticultural knowledge and writing and researching skills, and Gill, Jessica, Henry, and Chloe for their patience. Thanks also to Fran Suermondt and Lubera for their help, Simon Hickmott for his book *Growing Unusual Vegetables* that first inspired me to experiment many years ago, and to everyone at DK, particularly Alastair Laing and Stephanie Farrow for making this project happen.

Publisher's acknowledgements

Dorling Kindersley would like to thank Mark Winwood and his talented team of experienced growers for cultivating so many unusual crops from scratch and bringing their flair and enthusiasm to the project:

David Hall - *cabinet-maker and artist*
Alexis Datta - *retired Head Gardener at Sissinghurst Gardens, Kent*
Jacqui Ruthven - *retired Propagator at Sissinghurst Gardens, Kent*
Mandy Button - *owner of Stone Green Oast Holiday Accommodation, Stone in Oxney, Kent*

Thanks also to: Rosamund Cox, Jo Hargreaves, Emma Pinckard, Alison Shakespeare, Jane Simmonds, and Kathy Steer for editorial assistance; Anne Fisher, Glenda Fisher, and Jade Wheaton for design assistance; Myriam Mégharbi for picture research; Marie Lorimer for indexing; Steve Crozier for retouching images; and Kristopher Harper for his fuchsia berries.

Senior Editor Alastair Laing
Senior Art Editor Sara Robin
Designer Philippa Nash
Cover Design Steven Marsden
Pre-Production Producer Rebecca Fallowfield
Producer Stephanie McConnell
Managing Editor Stephanie Farrow
Managing Art Editor Christine Keilty
Art Director Maxine Pedliham
Publishing Director Mary-Clare Jerram

Photographer Mark Winwood

First published in Great Britain in 2018
by Dorling Kindersley Limited
80 Strand, London WC2R 0RL

Copyright © 2018 Dorling Kindersley Ltd

A Penguin Random House company
10 9 8 7 6 5 4 3 2 1
001–305960–Mar/2018

A CIP catalogue record for this book is available from the British Library.

ISBN 978-0-2413-0210-1

Printed and bound in China.

A WORLD OF IDEAS:
SEE ALL THERE IS TO KNOW
www.dk.com